THE AIT NDHIR OF MOROCCO:
A STUDY OF THE SOCIAL
TRANSFORMATION OF A BERBER TRIBE

Frontispiece: A settlement of the Ait Ndhir in the Middle Atlas Mountains.

ANTHROPOLOGICAL PAPERS

MUSEUM OF ANTHROPOLOGY, UNIVERSITY OF MICHIGAN

NO. 55

THE AIT NDHIR OF MOROCCO: A STUDY OF THE SOCIAL TRANSFORMATION OF A BERBER TRIBE

BY

AMAL RASSAM VINOGRADOV

ANN ARBOR

THE UNIVERSITY OF MICHIGAN, 1974

ACKNOWLEDGMENTS

I wish to thank the Center for Near Eastern and North African Studies for the financial support that made my field work possible, and for supporting the publication of this monograph. I feel a special debt of gratitude to the Director of the Center and my advisor, William D. Schorger, who introduced me to North African Studies and encouraged me throughout my graduate work at The University of Michigan.

Many people have contributed directly and indirectly to this study. I received invaluable advice and help from Eric Wolf, John Waterbury, Ernest Gellner, Rémy Leveau, David Hart, and Ernest Abdel-Massih. My fellow fieldworkers—Lawrence Rosen, Edmund Burke, and John Chiapuris—were very generous in sharing their ideas and field notes. To them all my sincere thanks.

Of the many Moroccans who helped me, I wish to single out Hajj Mohktar Amharesh and qaid Mohand n'Hamoucha of the Ait Ndhir. They graciously put up with my female presence in their jma'as and patiently made me understand and appreciate their vanished way of life.

I remember with great affection the women of the bled—Malika, Touria, Fadma and Amina—and all the others who took me in as a friend, confidante, and "sister." Their trust and concern made my stay less lonely.

To my husband and children, whose interest, encouragement, and sacrifice saw me through the difficult times, I dedicate this work.

A NOTE ON TRANSLITERATION

I have attempted to be both phonologically accurate and consistent without deviating too much from the French transliteration system that has become standard for Morocco. The deviations that do occur were felt to be necessary for the sake of accuracy, e.g., the Moroccan Arabic word for "army" has been transliterated in French literature as "guich." It appears in this study as "guish," a compromise for a better English transliteration. The author is aware of the fact that neither the form "guich" nor "guish" is really accurate. The correct form as heard in Morocco and as recorded on my field tapes is jish~žiš. However, to use this latter correct form at this time would lead to further confusion in an area already confused.

Correspondence of Modern Standard Arabic script and symbols used in the transcription

Symbol Used	Arabic Script
kh	خ
gh	غ
sh	ش
q	ق
j	ج
ʻ	ع
ṣ	ص
ḍ	ض
ḥ	ح
ʼ	ا
ṭ	ط

A PARTIAL GLOSSARY OF ARABIC TERMS*

'alem/'ulema/	religious savant
'askari/'askar/	soldiers
'azib	landholding, rural estate
baraka	quality of blessedness or holiness
bled ~ blad ~ bilad	countryside, country
ḍahir	imperial edict
dir	mountain slope
diyya	blood money
douar	rural settlement
fekhda/afkhad	lineage, clan, tribal segment
ferqa	tribal section
fqih	religious teacher
guish ~ guich ~ ar. jish	army
iqta'	land concession
khalifa	deputy
kharaj	land tax
leff ~ lleff	alliance
makhzan ~ makhzen	central government of Morocco
mulk	private property
qaḍi	religious judge
qaid	rural administrator
qsba ~ qaṣba	fortified town, citadel
shari'a ~ chrâa	Islamic religious law
sharif/shurfa/	descendant of the Prophet
siba	dissidence
souq ~ ssouq	market
tartib ~ tertib	agricultural tax
'urf	customary law
zawiya/zawaya/	religious order

*In this and the following glossary of Berber terms, plural forms are listed after a / line following their singular forms. The symbol ~ denotes a variant either in transliteration or form. The term Arabic, symbolized here as ar., refers to Moroccan Arabic.

A PARTIAL GLOSSARY OF BERBER TERMS

abrid	road, way; also, custom (ar. qa'ida)
agdal	pasture
akhatar/ikhataren/	old man, leader, large
amghar/imgharen/	tribal chief, war leader, notable
amur	pact of protection (ar. mezraq)
ḍalb~ḍḍalb	religious teacher
ighs/ikhsan/	tribal segment, clan
imagilla/imagillan/	co-juror (ar. ḥellaf)
izref	customary law (ar. 'urf)
jma'a	tribal assembly, meeting
taḍa	alliance
tagellat	collective oath
takhamt/tikhamen/	tent, household (ar. khima)
tamazirt	territory, country
tamghrost	sacrifice (ar. dbiḥa)
taryazt	courageous, independent, manly
taymat	brotherhood (ar. khuwa)
tazeltat	toll, fee
thamunt~tumint	alliance
tigemmi	tent group, community (ar. douar)
timizgida	mosque
tiwizi	corvée

TABLE OF CONTENTS

INTRODUCTION 1

I. FRENCH CONCEPTUAL FRAMEWORKS AND
   MOROCCAN REALITY 5
   The Makhzan-Siba Dichotomy 5
   The Phenomenon of Berberism 7

II. HISTORY OF THE AIT NDHIR 15
   The General Ethnohistorical Background 15
   The Nineteenth Century 20
   The Ait Ndhir and the Alawi Dynasty 21
   The Ait Ndhir at the Beginning of the Twentieth
      Century 26

III. ECOLOGY AND TRADITIONAL ECONOMIC
   ORGANIZATION 35
   The Ecological Setting 35
   The Tribal Territory 39
   Traditional Economy of the Ait Ndhir 42
   The Seasonal Migration 45
   Forms of Economic Cooperation 48

IV. SOCIOPOLITICAL ORGANIZATION 51
   Alternative Frameworks: Segmentation Versus
      Alliance 51
   What Was an Ait Ndhir Tribe? 54
   The Dynamics of Intra-Tribal Relationships .. 68
   Pacts of Brotherhood and Protection 72
   Violence and the Moral Order 75
   The Social Order of the Ait Ndhir: Concluding
      Remarks 77

V. THE DYNAMICS OF TRADITIONAL LAND TENURE AND TRIBAL ORGANIZATION ... 79

    The Makhzan Land Tenure System ... 79
    Guish and Naiba Tribes ... 81
    The 'Azib Institution ... 84
    Tribal Tenure: Collective Land ... 87
    Land Tenure and Land Use Among the Ait Ndhir ... 89
    The Ait Ndhir Tribe: An Adaptive Interpretation ... 91

VI. THE FRENCH PROTECTORATE AND LAND COLONIZATION ... 93

    French Order: The Legal Labyrinth ... 93
    The Case of the Ait Ndhir: "Un guich fictif" ... 96
    Unanticipated Consequences: Arabization and Residual Tribalism ... 100

VII. CONCLUSION ... 107

Appendix I ... 111
Appendix II ... 111
Appendix III ... 111
Appendix IV ... 112
Appendix V ... 112

Bibliography ... 115

Plates (following page 122)

LIST OF FIGURES

1. Map of principal historical migratory routes in Morocco ... 16
2. Sketch map of Morocco in the middle of the seventeenth century ... 22
3. A relief map of the Middle Atlas ... 36
4. Map illustrating major forms of economic adaptations in the Middle Atlas ... 37
5. Sketch map of the territory of the Ait Ndhir ... 40
6. Sketch map of tribal territory of the Ait Ndhir showing the distribution of the primary segments ... 41

TABLE OF CONTENTS

7. Sketch map indicating relative positions of the dir tribes during the transhumance cycle 43
8. The segmentary organization of the Ait Harzallah 58
9. Map of the guish tribes of the Alawi dynasty, including the "guich fictif" of the Ait Ndhir.................. 85
10. Cadastral map of the territorial division within the Ait Boubidman prior to 1912......................... 99
11. Cadastral map of the land ownership pattern prevailing in 1968 on the old territory of the Ait Boubidman 101

LIST OF PLATES
(Following page 122)

Frontispiece: A settlement of the Ait Ndhir in the Middle Atlas Mountains

1. A douar
2. An isolated household
3. A summer camp of the Ait Ndhir
4. Ait Ndhir tribesmen participating in a Fantasia
5. A ceremonial tent in the Middle Atlas Mountains
6. Holiday costume of an Ndhiri girl
7. The fqih and his family. Ait Harzallah
8. The former qaid of the Ait Ndhir and his wife in ceremonial dress
9. The Monday market near El-Hajeb
10. Market scene
11. The market near El-Hajeb
12. Going home from the market

INTRODUCTION

THE Ait Ndhir of the Middle Atlas is an enquiry into the nature of tribalism in Morocco and its historical relationship to the central government. Employing the Ait Ndhir as an example, this study attempts to establish a model for the traditional sociopolitical organization of a semi-nomadic Berber tribe of the Middle Atlas and examines the dynamics of the *makhzan*[1]-tribal symbiosis during the latter half of the 19th century. The last part of the study focuses on the impact of the French administration on the evolution of the Ait Ndhir, a transhumant Berber tribe located in the Meknes Plateau.

The tribe of the Ait Ndhir was selected because of the availability of a large body of ethnographic and historical material concerning the Fez-Meknes region. The bulk of this material has been published, and the rest is available in French Archives.[2] These data include detailed reports by French diplomats assigned to Fez before the establishment of the Protectorate as well as the accounts of various geographical and military missions that were sent to the area during the years between 1900 and 1915. This study is based on the foregoing written material and on data collected during six months of field work among the Ait Ndhir in 1968-1970.

There does not exist any complete work on the transhumant tribes of the Middle Atlas, with the exception of Ernest Gellner's book, *Saints of the Atlas* (see Chapter Four). The two outstanding works on Moroccan tribes are Jacque Berque's *Structures sociales du Haut Atlas* (Paris, 1955) and Robert Montagne's *Les Berbères et le makhzen dans le sud du Maroc* (Paris, 1930). Both of these studies describe the social organization of sedentary Berber cultivators in the western High Atlas. Until 1915 the Ait Ndhir were a

---

[1] The *makhzan* refers to the pre-Protectorate government of Morocco. The term was originally reserved for the treasury (*makhzan*, Arabic meaning storehouse), however, it was extended to include the total governmental apparatus. This usage began with the Almoravids (11th century) and persisted until Independence in 1956.

[2] The principal archives utilized for this study were those of the Ministère de la Guerre, section d'Afrique et d'Outre Mer, located at the Chateau de Vincennes.

pastoral people living in tents year round, despite the fact that they practiced some agriculture on the plain of the Sais.

Politically, the Ait Ndhir were what the Arab historians of Morocco call a ṭaraf tribe, from the Arabic *qaba'il al-ṭaraf*, the tribes at the edge. Beginning in 1860, the tribe was located at the edge of the effective limits of the makhzan's power, 50 kilometers from the royal cities of Fez and Meknes. Geographically close to the urban Arab culture, the Ait Ndhir, unlike other Berber speaking tribes (such as the Mjjat and Gerwan), maintained a remarkable purity in their institutions and language. There was very little Arabization.[3] It is as if their very position in the gallery overlooking the Arabized world of lowland Morocco and their political opposition to the guish tribes[4] who were protecting the Sais plain made them emphasize their "Berberism" and independence. This independence was made possible by obstinately maintaining their key institutions: semi-nomadism, communal ownership of land, and their own customary law (*izref*).[5] By resisting sedentarization and full-time agriculture on the plain, they also resisted incorporation into the exploitative network of the government. This "choice to be independent" expressed itself in the structural adaptation of the social group, the two major features of which were a complete absence of individual property in land and a high degree of flexibility and pragmatism in the application of the principles of tribal affiliation and cohesion.

The ebb and flow of the makhzan's power and effective domination in the area made for the emergence of a highly functional social organization, one trimmed to essentials and capable of accommodating several structural alternatives without loss of its basic nature. Strong sultans such as Mawlay Hassan (1875-1894) attempted to settle the tribe, to divide it into manageable administrative units for tax purposes, and to appoint non-tribal chiefs, *qaids*, to collect the tax. But as soon as Hassan died, the Ait Ndhir, taking

---

[3]This is not to deny that both ethnic groups shared a common metaphysical world view; if this were not the case, the Berbers would not have accepted the *shurfa* with their religious charisma (*baraka*) who came to play such a crucial role in the social structure of the tribes. This shared metaphysical outlook enabled the Berbers to accept the shurfa (or those who claimed such status) as mediators, healers, or advisors, and made of the Berber and Arab tribes a potential reservoir for dynasties.

[4]*Guish*, from the Arabic *jaysh* (army), referred to a number of tribes that were allied to the dynasty. Each family in the tribe supplied a combatant for the sultan's army. In return for this military service, the guish tribes were exempted from taxes. More detail on these tribes will follow.

[5]Attempts on the part of the makhzan to impose the Moslem law, *shari'a*, were perceived as a threat to the existence of the tribe, whose customary law, *izref* (Arabic *'urf*), was intimately bound up with their social structure and nomadic movements.

advantage of the chaotic interregnum period that usually followed the death of a sultan, rebelled against the imposed qaids, withheld their taxes, elected their own war leaders, and reverted to their favorite occupation, highway robbery.[6] This patterned instability (what the French elegantly called "stubborn anarchy") persisted until the French occupation of the region in 1912. Within years of their surrender and the establishment of a French administrative system, the distinctive aspects of the Ait Ndhir culture disappeared. This happened despite the deliberate policy and efforts of the French to keep the tribe as "Berber" as possible, or, in other words, to maintain the Berber language and distinctive institutions of the Ait Ndhir. The present condition of the tribe can be understood and explained properly only in terms of the changes initiated by the French. Of these, the most significant was the massive appropriation of tribal land which resulted in the transformation of the Berber from independent nomad to landless peasant and agricultural proletariat.

---

[6]The Ait Ndhir had a notorious reputation as bandits and rebels. They themselves admit to practicing banditry in times of the weakness of the makhzan. Their favored position astride both the internal Meknes-Marrakesh route and on the edge of the Meknes-Fez route rendered banditry lucrative. This outright banditry is not to be confused with the institutionalized protection *(mezraq)* which consisted of the payment of a toll tax by the travellers in tribal territory in return for their safety.

I
FRENCH CONCEPTUAL FRAMEWORKS AND MOROCCAN REALITY

THIS book seeks to question and attempts to rectify some of the generally accepted assumptions regarding the nature of tribalism in Morocco. These assumptions were the handiwork of French scholars who, until very recently, monopolized all enquiry into the ethnology and history of the country. In order to place the present study in its proper perspective, it is necessary to begin with a discussion of some of the dominant themes in the traditional French approach to Morocco.

THE MAKHZAN-SIBA DICHOTOMY

The French view of Morocco has been dominated by two major themes: tribal anarchy and Berberism. Both of these have been formulated in terms of antithetical dichotomies: *blad al makhzan* versus *blad al siba*,[1] and Arab versus Berber. These constructs were assumed to be of critical importance for the analysis and understanding of the nature and evolution of traditional Moroccan society. Consequently, the bulk of research has proceeded without questioning the validity or the utility of this dialectic approach which, it must be admitted, is a seductive one since it circumvents the conceptual and methodological difficulties inherent in any attempt to deal comprehensively with the complex and confusing flux of Moroccan history.

---

[1] Literally "the land of government and the land of dissidence." Incidentally, the Ait Ndhir never spoke in terms of an *area* of tribal dissidence but rather in terms of a *state* of dissidence. The following incident from my field notes may illustrate their attitude: I was interviewing an old Ndhiri one morning, when two rural policemen, *mkhaznis*, came to arrest the man and take him to jail. The policeman explained to me that the old tribesman had failed to comply with the orders of the local *qaid*. The *qaid* had asked several Ndhiri men to take their horses and tents to a nearby resort town in order that they may participate in a "spontaneous tribal celebration" in honor of the birthday of his majesty King Hassan II. As the old Ndhiri was led away, he complained that it was harvest time, and that he had no desire to leave his work and go and "dance and ride the horses for the sultan." He then turned to me and said, "God bless the days of the *siba, Allah yerham essiba*," to which the policeman replied, "The *siba* is dead forever, you old fool."

The makhzan-siba approach has dominated the work of French historians (including the eminent Henri Terrasse), who have viewed Moroccan history within the framework of a continual conflict between the Arab makhzan and the anarchic Berber tribes. One consequence of this view has been to consider the makhzan as an "État manqué" because of its failure to establish political control over all the tribes within the geographical confines of the country. Another consequence has been the tendency to interpret the makhzan-tribal contest as the struggle of civilization against the barbarian hordes.

Any rigidly formalistic approach to the sociopolitical history of Morocco has the tendency to oversimplify and ultimately obfuscate both the nature of the traditional forms of social organization and the pattern of accommodations that prevailed among the different segments of the society. These segments included tribes, zawiyas, 'ulemas, shurfa, and urban guilds.[2] An examination of the symbiotic relationship that prevailed between the segments and between the makhzan and the segments, may help to explain the remarkable resiliency exhibited by the traditional sociopolitical system as a whole. This kaleidoscopic system persisted essentially unchanged from its initiation by the Sa'adi dynasty (16th century) to the establishment of the French Protectorate in 1912.

A shift in the focus of analysis from the opposition between makhzan and tribe to an examination of the operational norms and procedures that permitted the co-existence of government and anarchy within one system, has been evident in two recent works on Morocco: Stuart Schaar's *Conflict and Change in 19th Century Morocco* (1965) and John Waterbury's *The Commander of the Faithful, The Moroccan Political Elite: A Study in Segmented Politics* (1970). This holistic and dynamic approach to the political culture of traditional Morocco is based on the assumption that:

> ... the makhzan had only a relative monopoly of coercive means within the country. Moreover, what power it did have was not institutionalized and varied from one sultan to another. It was delegated, contingent power. Groups which were its retainers of first instance, tribes, shurafa', local big men, 'ulema, accepted that the power that they and their followers represented be used towards generally specific ends on the basis of generally specific pacts. The power of the sultan consisted of the sum total of the power of his momentary allies at any one time. The sultan provided a convenient rallying point and a widely accepted religious authority, around which various interests could form in the light of their

---

[2] *'Ulema* (sing. *'alem*) are religious savants. *Shurfa* (sing. *sharif*) are descendants of the Prophet. *Zawiya* (pl. *zawaya*) refer to a religious brotherhood.

own, rapidly changing interests. The particular configuration of makhzan allies was often transformed more than once even during the sultan's lifetime: enemies became allies, became enemies again, and so on. Most political actors were fully aware of the inevitability of these fluctuations, and thus avoided placing exclusive moral judgments on rival groups and personalities. The definition of local, immediate interest determined the choice of a faction's allies. 'Tensions were institutionalized in such a way that enemies could not destroy one another without ruining themselves. The result was the role of "live and let live" which defined relations among antagonists' (Waterbury, 1970:29-30).

The present study approaches the history of the Ait Ndhir within the above framework and seeks to show that tribalism was neither a survival from an early and primitive stage of history nor a marginal and insignificant phenomenon confined to remote regions of the Sharifian Empire. Tribalism in its many variations was an integral part of the total Moroccan social and historical experience. Given the arbitrary and exploitative nature of the makhzan, the tribal framework provided a viable and secure structure for the recruitment and organization of groups, distribution of resources, and management of local conflict.

THE PHENOMENON OF BERBERISM

The second grand theme in French literature on Morocco is "Le berbèrisme." French ethnologists have traditionally assumed that the division of Moroccan society into Arabs and Berbers constituted its single most significant characteristic. "Arab" and "Berber" were viewed as mutually exclusive categories, each composed of a relatively homogeneous group of people.[3] The French failed to see that the differences between what constitutes an Arab and what constitutes a Berber are very subtle and that the importance of ethnic identification varies with the situational context as well as with the additional affiliations by which each person is characterized at any particular moment.[4] Hence, a person may be more Arab and less Berber at one time, and more Berber and less Arab at another. Ethnic identity is neither clear-cut nor exclusive in Morocco, and the Arab-Berber categories are rarely perceived by the

---

[3]The stereotype of the corporate Berber ethnic identity is unfortunately not limited to French ethnographers. Contemporary Arab urban elite tend to agree with Jean Lacouture that "to be Berber is, quite simply, to be not quite yet Arabized. . . . Perhaps only one trait is common to all the Berber speakers: the taste for opposition, above all, verbal; for contradictory debate. This hardly facilitates the formation of a constant and constructive policy towards them" (Lacouture, 1958:83, 86).

[4]For a recent consideration of the relevance and function of ethnic identity in Morocco, see Lawrence Rosen (1973).

individuals themselves as being mutually exclusive. Failure to appreciate this institutionalized ambivalence regarding ethnicity leads to the confusion and dilemma experienced by French political officers faced by the seemingly inconsistent attitudes of "nos berbères." In 1948, at the graduation ceremonies of the local school of El Hajeb, the administrative center of the Ait Ndhir tribe, a Berber boy from the Ait Ndhir recited a speech in classical Arabic. Much to the surprise and confusion of the French teachers and political officers present, the speech became the highlight of the program that had included French poetry, Berber folk dances, and Ndhiri legends. The French were puzzled by the reaction of the Berbers who were present; for despite the fact that only a few understood what was said in the speech, all of them expressed great pride and contentment that a local boy had mastered the language of the Quran.

As Jacques Berque wrote, "The analysis of Maghrib societies requires, not a distinction between what may be 'Berber,' 'Arab,' or 'French,' but criteria that would trace, with respect to the Maghrib personality, the greater or lesser coherence or dynamism achieved in the integration of heterogeneous characteristics and in the response of the group to its milieu" (1966:194). In order to fully appreciate the genesis and significance of the Arab-Berber distinction in Moroccan scholarship, a brief foray into the history of French ethnology in Morocco is necessary.[5]

French Ethnology: The Early Years

Moroccan social scientists are currently engaged in a concerted effort to decolonize the concepts and intellectual constructs that have determined the selection and interpretation of Moroccan data in the last 50 years.[6] For, in Morocco, more than anywhere else in North Africa, ethnology was the handmaiden of colonial politics. From the early days of the Protectorate, and under the directorship of the first resident-general, Marshall Louis Lyautey, social research established itself as a veritable political institution and a branch of colonial public administration. As the Moroccan sociologist Abdelkabir Khatibi wrote, "Dès la debut de la colonisation au Moroc, la sociologie fut organisée dans un esprit utilitaire et dans un objectif d'application; à sa manière, la sociologie preparait la

---

[5] The ensuing account of French ethnology in Morocco is largely based on Nicolas (1961: 527-543).

[6] Among these Moroccan social scientists, native and naturalized, are Abdelkabir Khatibi, Ahmad Naciri, Ahmad Lahlimi, Paul Pascon, and Grigori Lazarev.

'pacification' et épaulait l'administration; la politique, de son cité, dirigeat et orientait la recherche" (1969:9).

In 1904 A. Le Chetelier, professor of "Moslem sociology" at the College de France, founded the "Mission Scientifique" Institute in Tangier. The object of the institute was to gather social and political data in anticipation of the French military occupation. In 1907 the "Mission Scientifique" was placed under the direction of E. Michaux-Bellaire who was assisted by G. Salmon. Aided by a large and heterogeneous group of researchers, the two Frenchmen managed to collect an impressive amount of data on all facets of Moroccan life. The bulk of this data was published as the *Archives berbères (1915-1920)* and as the collection, *Tribus et villes du Maroc*.

Influenced by the attitude of the aristocratic Marshall Lyautey, who had a horror of direct administration and a certain respect for traditional institutions, French colonial policy for the years between 1912 and 1925 was ambiguous and lacked a definite program for tribal populations. Michaux-Bellaire, however, soon set the style for future policy. He proposed the division of Moroccan social enquiry into three distinct categories: "sociologie makhzan," "sociologie musulmane," and "sociologie marocaine."[7] By "sociologie marocaine" Michaux-Bellaire meant the study of the original beliefs and institutions of the indigenous inhabitants of Morocco: the Berbers. Michaux-Bellaire believed that it was both possible and important to identify and isolate the purely Berber values and institutions from the Arab-Islamic context in which they had become embedded.

The assumption of the existence of a separate Berber personality and culture was reflected in a belief that was widely held by Protectorate officials, that the Berber was potentially assimilable to French civilization in contrast to the Moroccan Arab. The departure of Marshall Lyautey in 1925 allowed the introduction of a frankly racist and separatist colonial policy, one designed to isolate the Berbers and insulate them from the greater Arab cultural context of Morocco. This policy culminated in the promulgation of the notorious "Berber ḍahir" of May 16, 1930. The edict affirmed in public what had been a general practice under both the makhzan and the French, namely the right of local tribunals to administer their own tribal customary law, izref, in areas considered

---

[7] E. Michaux-Bellaire originally proposed this division in a lecture he gave to a group of Officers des Affaires Indigenes. Parts of his speech were later published as "La sociologie marocaine," *Archives Marocaines*, vol. 27, 1927, pp. 293-311. See also E. Michaux-Bellaire, *La mission scientifique du Maroc*, Service de Renseignements, Rabat, 1925, 22 pages.

"purely Berber." This meant that certain communities were "legally" removed from the jurisdiction of the formal Islamic law, shari'a which applied to the rest of the country.[8] The outraged reaction to this blatant colonial separatist maneuver contributed to the consolidation and expansion of the national movement in the country.[9]

The Colonizing Ethnologist: Robert Montagne

The intellectual heir to Michaux-Bellaire and the most influential ethnologist in Morocco was Robert Montagne. A naval officer, Montagne was recruited by Marshall Lyautey to study the then rebellious tribes of the south of Morocco. The French had by that time completed the pacification of the plains and were in the process of conquering piecemeal the Berber-speaking tribes of the Atlas mountains.

Montagne reduced Michaux-Bellaire's three categories to two: "sociologie makhzan" and "sociologie berbère." "Le berbèrisme" was no longer an idea to be demonstrated; with Montagne it became an accepted postulate. Impressed by the fighting spirit of the mountain warriors, and attracted by their "unspoiled primitivism," Montagne developed a colonially patronizing attitude toward the Berbers. "Peut-être n'est-il pas temeraire d'espérer qu'un jour viendra ou les tribus de montagne, dont le territoire dessiné sur la bordure de l'ancien 'bled el Makhzen' de vastes regions naturelles, pourront, grâce à notre appui, s'affranchir, dans une certaine mesure, des liens trop étroits dans lesquels les ensèrre aujourd'hui la tradition chérifiènne. Dans ces provinces eloignées des villes, dont l'histoire du pays suffit à tracer assez exactement les limites, les Berbères prendront conscience avec plus du force, sous un regime administratif adapté à leur existence, des liens si durables qui les unissent à leur sol" (1930:419).

Montagne became fascinated with what he termed the "astonishing contradictions" in Berber tribal society. These contradictions consisted of the fact that on the one hand "les tribus sédentaires ou nomades de la Berbérie . . . s'attachent à faire respecter dans leurs États primitifs des institutions démocratiques ou oligarchiques . . . d'autre part, nous savons qu'il s'est toujours élevé, au sein de ces

---

[8] The artificiality of affirming the customary tribunals only in areas considered Berber is evident from the fact that Arab tribes also have tribunals who administer the customary law, 'urf, which is often at variance with the shari'a. In other words, customary law is not a Berber phenomenon.

[9] Detailed information on the "Berber dahir," regional administration of Berber areas, and general French policy to Berbers is to be found in Stephane Bernard (1963).

tribus, fidèles à leurs lois traditionnelles, partagées en miniscules républiques, des chefs de principautés capables de briser par leurs propres forces toutes les résistances, de constituer en quelques années de vastes commandements et même de fonder des dynasties" (1930:vii). Montagne's theory of the rise and fall of these petty chiefdoms, *qaidats*, constitutes his major contribution to the study of Moroccan tribal structure. His explanation is partly predicated on the assumption that the major factor favoring the maintenance and stability of tribal structure is the presence of an extensive and permanent alliance system, the *leff*. According to Montagne, the formation and dissolution of the micro-states in the western High Atlas is a result of the state of unstable equilibrium in which the Berber tribes exist. This unstable equilibrium is a result of the opposition between the tribal desire for independence and the centralizing influence of the makhzan.

Despite all his experience and knowledge, Montagne's cultural myopia led him to misconstrue the nature and the evolution of Moroccan society. During World War II he collaborated with General G. Catroux to develop a program whose aim was to maintain French hegemony over Northwest Africa. The program recommended partial reforms and greater flexibility in the colonial administrative framework with limited integration of national elite. These halfhearted measures proved no panacea for the Protectorate, as the events of the fifties proved.

Montagne represented the epitome of the contradictions inherent in the French attitude towards Berbers: what was originally a potentially assimilable group became an "indigène" to be pitied: "Il est difficile, lorsqu'on mesure la vanité des résultats obtenus par le Makhzen . . . pendant dix siècles de luttes, d'échapper à un sentiment de pitié a l'égard de ce peuple réduit a une servitude sans idéal, dans une misère sans espoir, et qui ne cherche plus de remède à ses maux que par un retour impuissant et passager à lanarchie d'autrefois" (1930:391).

A Contemporary Approach: Jacques Berque

A new phase in the study of rural Morocco began with the work of Jacques Berque. An Algerian born Frenchman, of sharp sensitivity and uncanny empathy, Berque has almost singlehandedly sought to decolonize his compatriots' approaches to Morocco and the Arab world in general.

Following World War II, Berque witnessed the efforts of the

French Protectorate to deal with the sharp increase in population, mass unemployment, and the accelerated rural-urban migration. He was a member of the Secteurs de Modernisation de Paysannat (1945-47), an agency hastily set up by the French whose objective was to increase the agricultural production in the countryside. This it proposed to do through a massive effort to modernize the *fellah* (peasant). (This was a marked reversal of colonial policy which had previously sought to maintain the fellah as "traditional" as possible.) Model farms were created on tribal land that was leased by the government; these farms were to serve as examples and nuclei for future cooperatives to be owned and run by the tribesmen themselves.[10] In order to prepare the fellah for the shock of exchanging the mule for the tractor, a massive educational and "psychological" program accompanied the undertaking. However, the whole experiment met with failure. It was resisted by the sullen and confused fellah and the European colon who suspected a plot to undermine his privileged position.

After leaving the Paysannat, Berque was assigned to the region of Marrakesh and while there he embarked on the research that resulted in the finest book on tribal North Africa: *Structures sociales du Haut Atlas* (Paris, 1955). Berque abandoned the Arab-Berber categories of his predecessors and concentrated on the understanding of what he termed "the bewildering contrasts" evident in rural Morocco. He underscored the dynamism and flexibility of tribal structures as well as the ambiguity of social relationships. He believed that this social ambiguity and structural resiliency were responsible for the remarkable ability of Moroccan tribes to combine simultaneously the elements of an open society and a closed corporate one. In his study of the Seksawa of the High Atlas, Berque demonstrated that even though the Berbers took refuge in the mountains, their dependence on the outside world did not decrease. Tribal law was administered by the Arab shurfa, who mediated conflict, and economically the tribes were interlocked into an ever-expanding network of rural markets that encompassed much more than a simple local exchange. According to Berque, it is both futile and foolish to attempt to separate what is Moslem from what is genuinely Berber in Morocco, for Islam had spread into every crevice of the country, altering and adapting itself to local conditions.

---

[10]The work of the Paysannat among the Ait Ndhir represented an interesting reversal in policy. After introducing private property, *mulk*, among the tribe which up until the Protectorate had owned its land communally, the French were now asking tribesmen to think in terms of owning shares in land, that is to say, cooperative farming.

Believing that one of the fundamental properties of Islam is its ability to embrace contradictions, Berque is currently engaged in examining the different forms of cultural synthesis that are being worked out throughout the Arab world, his major focus being on the problem of cultural identity and modernization. Berque writes in a rich and dialectical style full of symbolic and historical references and his range of interest is astounding. It may not be captious to say that, at this stage, Berque's work remains more suggestive than definitive. But it was largely due to his effort that the colonially constructed edifice of Moroccan ethnology was undermined.[11]

---

[11] For a more detailed history and evaluation of French social science in Morocco, see Berque (1956:296-324).

II
HISTORY OF THE AIT NDHIR

THIS chapter begins with a general synthetic account of the ethnohistory of the Ait Ndhir and proceeds to a more detailed description of the interaction of the tribe with the Alawi dynasty. The last section is devoted to the French military pacification of the region and the resistance of the Ait Ndhir during the years 1910-1913.

THE GENERAL ETHNOHISTORICAL BACKGROUND

The Ait Ndhir, whose Arabic name is Beni Mtir,[1] form one of the Sanhaja Berber tribes of the Middle Atlas. Ibn-Khaldun (1956-60) divided the Berber speaking population of North Africa into three main divisions: the Masmuda, the Sanhaja, and the Zenata. He then proceeded to describe each of these divisions for Morocco. The Masmuda comprised the original population of the country; they occupied the western part, namely the Rif, PreRif, and the Jbala. They also constituted the majority of the inhabitants of the western High Atlas and the Anti Atlas, and shared the Atlantic plain with the Bergrouatas and the Regraga. They were predominantly sedentary cultivators.

The Sanhaja originated in the southern part of Morocco and gradually gained a foothold in the Eastern and Central Atlas. Predominantly pastoralists, they searched for better pastures and slowly infiltrated the Middle Atlas as far as the Oued Oum Al Rabia. Arab historians refer to them as the traditional and hereditary enemies of the Masmuda. In the south of Morocco, they formed a separate class that dominated the oases and ruled over the sedentary agricultural groups known collectively as *harattin*.

---

[1] The linguistic duality of the name of the tribe expresses its cultural and geographic position at the juncture of the Arab and Berber zones. They now refer to themselves as the Beni Mtir or Mtiris, adding occasionally that this is the Arab version of their real Berber name: Ait Ndhir. In other contexts, however, they will "prove" their Arab origins and affiliations by pointing out the existence of an Arab tribe called the Beni Mtir in Tunis of which they claim they once formed a part.

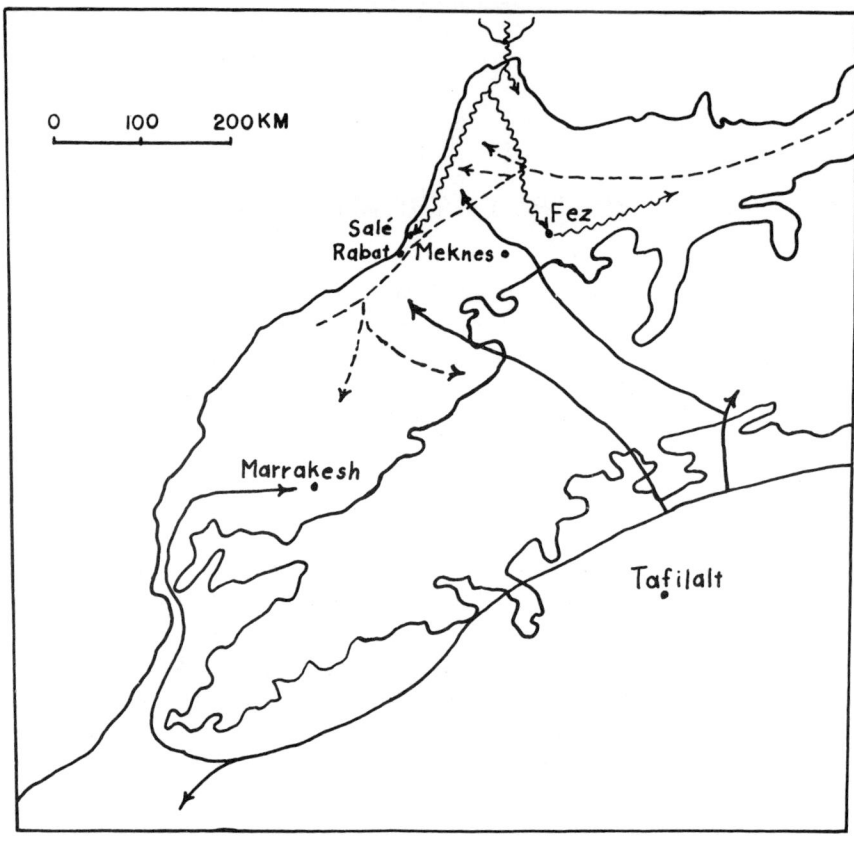

- - - ▶ Beni Hilal invasion in the 12th century.
⎯⎯⎯▶ Beni Ma'aqil invasion in the 13th century.
∿∿∿▶ Arab and Jewish migrants from Andalus in the 15th century.

Fig. 1. Rough map showing the principal historical migratory routes.

The Zenata are known to be the last arrivals on the Moroccan scene. Coming from the east, some of them occupied the Sebou and Moulouya valleys. They bypassed Fez and founded Miknasat al-Zeitoun (today Meknes).

Ibn-Khaldun characterizes the Sanhaja as that Berber group which did not contribute a dynasty to Morocco. He estimates that by the fourteenth century, they had already reached the Middle Atlas, but that the real avalanche of the Sanhaja movement in a northwesterly direction did not begin until the end of the seventeenth century. This massive migration brought the Berbers in direct contact with the makhzan and it is in this era that the Middle Atlas tribes appear in the political history of Morocco. It is highly likely that the Sanhaja started out from the Sahara on a northerly migration route seeking better pastures, water, and shade. All traditions in the Middle Atlas refer vaguely to a Saharan origin, but otherwise the Middle Atlas region is rather poor in legends referring to specific origins.

A survey of the dominant traditions indicates that all the different groups of the Middle Atlas are arranged in one of two ways: on the basis either of ethnic origins or political alliances.

The first tradition attributes a common ancestor to them all. According to this legend, all the *tamazight*-speaking Berbers[2] descend from Jalout (Goliath) who lived a thousand years before Jesus and who was killed by David (Sidna Daoud). Jalout left behind four sons, one of whom, Baidi, was murdered by the Arabs while still an infant, thus giving origin to the enmity between the Arabs and the Berbers. Each of the other three sons (Molou, Midoul, Atta) became the ancestor of a tamazight group.[3]

Malou

Abou al Kassem Ezzayani	founder of the Zayan
Al Yazid al Shqirni	founder of the Ishqern
Mohammed al Youssi	founder of the Youssi
Brahim al Sokhmani	founder of the Sokhman
Sheikh al Mekki al Mguildi	founder of the Mguild
Saddine Yemmour	founder of the Beni Sadden

Midoul

Yanhia	founder of the Ait Yahia
Agra	founder of the Guerouan
Morghad	founder of the Morghad
Hadidou	founder of the Hadidou
Ymour	founder of the Ymour

Atta

Hlim	ancestor of people of the Dra Valley
Azza	ancestor of people of the Magha
Khilifa	ancestor of people of the Annebghi
Khabbash	ancestor of people of the Ait Khabbash
Sfoul	ancestor of people of the Ait Sfoul
Mtir	ancestor of people of the Ait Ndhir

[2]Tamazight refers to one of three Berber dialects in Morocco, the other two being Rifi and Tashilhit. The term tamazight means "free" and Middle Atlas Berbers refer to themselves as *"imazighin"* or free men. The Arab speaking people refer to all Berbers of the Middle Atlas regardless of dialect and origin as *"shleuh."*

[3]There exist many versions of the legend of Jalout, no two are exactly alike. The Ait Ndhir have a very simple version which will be presented later on in the study. One version of the legend was found in manuscript form in zawiya sidi bou Yacoub near the city of Tafilalet (see Guennoun, 1939:209-223).

The second attempt at classifying the tamazight tribes is a more historical one and is based on grouping them into political confederations. This grouping of tribes into larger and more inclusive sets is always resorted to by older informants as they try to recall the movements of the tribal groups. However, they seldom agree on the precise composition of these superconfederations. The confusion and disagreement no doubt reflect the highly fragile and ephemeral nature of the majority of political alliances that changed in time and with circumstances. There is, however, an overall agreement that the following three super-confederations prevailed for a long time and were most important: Ait Oumalou, Ait Yafelman, and Ait Idrassen.[4] The Ait Oumalou (literally "people of the shade or shadow") represented those tribes which in the eighteenth century were found on the northern slopes of the High Atlas. Their solidarity was sporadic and expressed itself mainly in joint opposition to the expansion of the Ait Atta from the south and the occasional makhzan penetration from the north (see Dunn, 1969). Originally grouped into the Ait Oumalou were the following tribes: Ishqern, Beni Mguild, Ishaq, Zayan, and Ait Sokhamn. The Ait Yafelman (literally "those who found peace") incorporated a number of tribes located at the southern end of the High Atlas around Midelt. They pastured in the high mountains (maximum altitude 3000 meters for Jebel Ayashi) and utilized the pastures in the valleys of Ziz and Gheris in the winter. They comprised the Ait Yahia, Ait Hadidou, Ait Morghad, Ait Izdig, and the Gerwan.

Finally, there was the Ait Idrassen whose origins and composition are most obscure. For today, whereas the memory of the Oumalou and Yafelman are still very much alive and groups are still identified through affiliation with these superconfederations, there is very little recollection of the Idrassen. This may reflect the fact that, of the three, it alone suffered a shattering military defeat and dismemberment at the hands of Mawlay Hassan. The French priest-missionary, Charles de Foucould, relates a legend he heard while traveling in the Middle Atlas in 1883 to the effect that all the Ait Idrassen share a common ancestor called Yacoub ben Daoud ben Idrassen (1939:43). Actually, the Ait Idrassen was a paramilitary grouping of diverse tribes who were on the plains of the High Moulouya and who at the end of the eighteenth century banded together to defend their living space against the encroaching tribes

---

[4]The term *ait* is the Berber segmentary prefix par excellence and is equivalent to the Arabic *Beni*. Both mean "sons of," "people of" and as with the Arabic term, *ait* is used throughout the segmentary scale regardless of size or inclusiveness.

from the south. One version has the Ait Idrassen composed of Ait Ihand, Ait Ayash, Ouafella, Youssi, Beni Mtir, and the Mjatt. The Ayash, Ihand, and Ouafella settled to cultivation in the high plains of Midelt; the Ait Youssi were "on horseback" patrolling the routes of passage in the valleys of the Upper Moulouya, while the Mtir and Mjatt were moving between the valleys of the Moulouya and the high plateau of Azrou.

Local traditions mention a period of drought, *qaht*, that is held responsible for the migrations in the Middle Atlas. More probably, continuous periods of drought, famine, and population growth taxed the limited resources of the oasis and the dry steppes in the south and resulted in a continual push to the northwest. The endless migratory movements of pastoral peoples, both Arab and Berber, is a major theme in the history of Morocco. The most famous and dramatic thrust was that of Almoravids who exploded out of the Mauritanian desert to initiate one of the most glorious periods in the dynastic history of the country.

The end of the seventeenth century must have witnessed an extended period of drought and famine in the south which initiated the accelerated migrations that carried the Ait Ndhir to the outskirts of the royal cities of Fez and Meknes. Jostled by the Ait Atta at the Saharan end and afflicted with drought and famine, the movement of the tribes was amplified in all the Middle Atlas.[5] Needless to say these mass migrations were uneven both in tempo and scale. A segment of a tribe would push and replace another either through treaty or force. This explains the continually changing territorial pattern of the Moroccan tribes and makes historical identification a very difficult and hazardous game.

Unable to impose its hegemony in the area of the Middle Atlas, the central government sought to act as a lever. Directly or through the shurfa, who often acted as agents, sultans interfered in the tribal alliances. They sought to break up the potentially powerful confederations and cement splinter groups to act as buffers in strategic areas. Often, following a military victory over a rebellious tribe, the makhzan would have the tribal group dismembered and the parts relocated in different areas of the empire. This procedure of the government was known as *naql*, transfer.

---

[5] Rainfall pattern is very erratic in this part of the country. Periodic dessication of pasture forces tribes to move up the mountains.

THE NINETEENTH CENTURY

At the beginning of the nineteenth century, the Ait Idrassen seem to have been firmly installed in the region of the Upper Moulouya. Powerful pastoral tribes stretched from the north to the south exploiting complementary vegetation zones that included part of the High Atlas, plains of the Moulouya, and the fringes of the Middle Atlas. The Ait Youssi were found between Midelt and the plain of Enjil encircling the massif of Tichoukt. The Ait Ouafella were on the piedmont of Midelt around the oasis of Bertat where they are still found today. The Ait Ndhir were between oued Guercif and oued Bou Dadjoul in the region of Itzer. Thus the Ait Idrassen were really the political expression of a number of groups utilizing adjacent territory. The Ait Mguild, meanwhile, had wedged themselves in the hollow of the Aghbalou-n-Serdane between the Ihand and the Ait Ndhir. In order not to be engulfed by the Idrassen, and being in direct competition with them for pasture space, the Mguildis sought to maintain contact with their Ait Oumalou allies, the Ait Sokhman, found then on the border of Oued al Abid. This meant continual fighting with the Ihand who were in the way.

In 1803, the Sultan, Mawlay Sliman, judged the Ait Idrassen to be too powerful. He started a series of military campaigns that resulted in the defeat of the Idrassen and the disruption of the established tribal pattern in the Upper Moulouya region. The Ait Ayash were dismembered: one section, known as the Ait Oufellah, was incorporated with the Ait Mguild and another was transferred and relocated near Fez.[6] The rest of the Ait Ayash were driven back to the Ansegmir valley where they are found today. The Ait Ndhir retreated to the Guigou valley, while the Ait Mguild, taking advantage of the vacuum left by the dispersal of the Idrassen, occupied the territory between Agercif and the plain of Enjil. It should be pointed out that in this heaving sea of Berber migrations and chronic fighting, there existed small peaceful islands of sedentary Arab cultivators. All these groups claimed sharifian descent and the majority lived off their traditional roles as conflict mediators and as dispensers of divine charisma, *baraka*.[7]

Out of the chaos of the second half of the nineteenth century, a semblance of stability and a pattern of tribal adaptation was be-

---

[6] This section of the Ait Ayash is still found near Fez today. Following their relocation from the upper Moulouya, the isolated tribal clan was registered by the government as a guish tribe.

[7] For the role and structure of one of these groups in the central High Atlas, see E. Gellner (1969).

ginning to emerge. This took the following general form: along the western and central parts of the Middle Atlas, tribes were settled in small fortified villages, *qsours*, in the midst of their fields. Large empty areas separated the different tribes. On the northern and northwestern borders of the Middle Atlas range, pastoral tribes were seeking larger and still better pastures for their animals and lived in a state of continual conflict over the shifting boundaries. This fighting was occasionally relieved by the alliances that were forged to protect the weaker tribes and neutralize the stronger ones.

THE AIT NDHIR AND THE ALAWI DYNASTY

This section will focus on the interaction of the Ait Ndhir with the Alawi makhzan. Even though the tribe does not emerge as a separate, named, political entity until the middle of the eighteenth century, it was consistently singled out from the Idrassen confederation and identified as a powerful tribe. The following account is based primarily on Ahmad Al-Nasiri (1954-59).[8]

From the Inception of the Dynasty to Mawlay Hassan

The Sultan Ahmad Al-Mansour died in 1603 and his death ushered in a protracted period of weakness and anarchy that resulted in the expiration of the Sa'di dynasty when the Sultan Al-Abbas was assassinated in 1628. As was usual, rival claimants to the throne were competing in the different sections of the country, and the northern areas were being invaded by England, Spain, and Portugal. Since the makhzan was unable to meet the challenge of the infidel, the task of inspiring and organizing the *jihad* (holy war) fell into the hands of the different *murabitin* and the zawiyas.[9] The political influence and role of the zawiyas (especially on the national scale) tended to be inversely proportional to the strength of the makhzan.

By 1630, the shifting political scene had stabilized into three major zones of influence, each dominated by a different zawiya. The Dila ruled in the northern part of the country, while the Alawis of Tafilalet shared the southern and western areas with the Semlali zawiya.

The Dila zawiya was founded among the Berber Mjjat tribe of

---
[8] Especially volumes VIII and IX.

[9] A *murabit* (French marabout) is a man whose sancitity is acquired through the gift of divine grace and a life consecrated to religion. *Zawiya* is a religious brotherhood or fraternity. These brotherhoods were usually founded by the *murabitin*.

the Middle Atlas. The history of this zawiya is an example of a persistent theme in Moroccan history (see Drague, 1951, and Mohammad Hajji, 1964). Even though the origins of the founder were among the Mjjat, Sidi Abu Bekr, who was a famous murabit, claimed

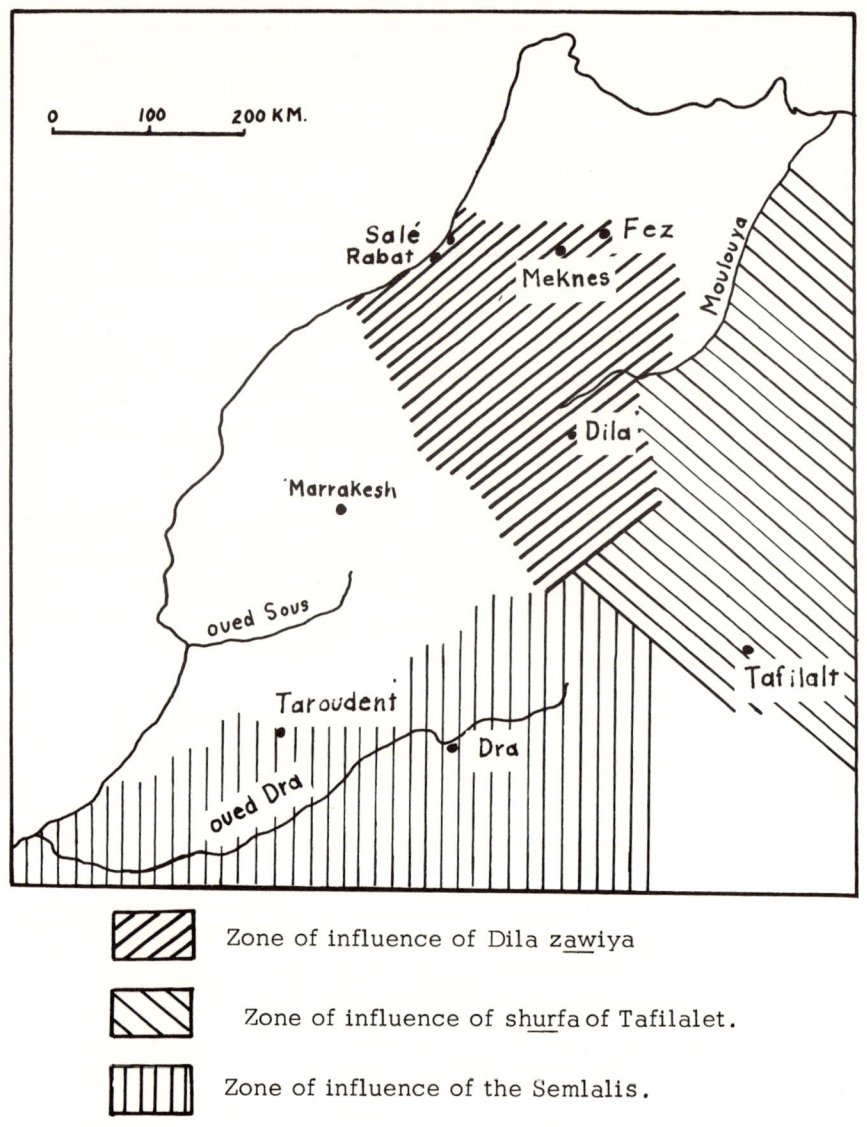

Zone of influence of Dila zawiya

Zone of influence of shurfa of Tafilalet.

Zone of influence of the Semlalis.

Fig. 2. Morocco in the middle of the 17th century (map adapted from André Julien, *Histoire de l'Afrique du Nord*, p. 221).

sharifian status for himself. One of his descendants, Mohammad Al-Hajj, took advantage of the weakness of the Sa'di dynasty, preached the jihad against the Portuguese and succeeded in forging the Middle Atlas nomadic tribes into a coherent fighting army. With this army at his command, Al-Hajj established a political domain that extended from the Middle Atlas to Rabat and Salé on the Atlantic coast. Among the tribes that formed the core of the Dila army were the Ait Ndhir, Ymmour, and the Ayash. The Dila shurfa stayed in power until they were defeated by the Filali sharif, Mawlay Al-Rashid in 1668. The Dila lodge was burned down and the order was scattered.

Mawlay Al-Rashid, the founder of the Alawi dynasty, was succeeded by his brother Ismael who assumed the sultanate at the age of 26 (1672-1727). Sultan Ismael set out to consolidate and expand the domain of the new dynasty. Having established his hegemony over the tribes on the plains, he turned to the mountains. Leading a powerful army, he went to the Upper Moulouya and Jebel Ayashi where he spent one year. On his way back, he built the *qasbas* of Azrou and Ain Leuh. He succeeded in cutting the winter route of the nomadic Idrassen and obliged them to accept peace and pay an indemnity in horses and arms and encouraged them to settle and cultivate the soil. But the makhzan's victory lasted only as long as the army remained in the area, for, after the death of Mawlay Ismael, the Berbers regained their independence.

During the reign of Mawlay Abdallah (1727-1757), the Idrassen again became powerful and were united under the supreme command of Mohammad ou Aziz of the Ait Ndhir. Al-Nasiri wrote that the Sultan paid ou Aziz a stipend to keep the tribes in check, and, that sometime later, following a palace coup by the 'Abid (a black praetorian guard), Mawlay Abdallah sought refuge among the Idrassen. But this entente was short-lived. In time, the Sultan allied himself with the Gerwan tribe who were in direct competition for pasture with the Idrassen. Aided by the Oudaya, a guish tribe, the Gerwan defeated the Idrassen near the town of Azrou. A section of the Idrassen, the Ait Ndhir, sent a delegation to the Sultan seeking *aman*, or safety. This procedure of seeking peace or safety is a ritualized one: a delegation of tribal notables bearing gifts and sacrificial animals would ask for an audience with the Sultan. During the audience, they would all declare their desire for peace and pledge their political allegiance to the person of the Sultan.

The Sultan granted the Ait Ndhir his aman and agreed to settle a section of them south of Meknes, after they agreed to be governed by a qaid appointed by the Sultan. This marked the first appearance of the Ait Ndhir on the plain. From this period on the tribe appears in the forefront of the dynastic struggles for succession. These often became contests between the different pretenders and their champions among the guish tribes, 'ulema, and the nearby Berber tribes. During the years 1810-1820, the Ait Ndhir participated in what the French refer to as "la Revolte Berbère." Incited by a charismatic leader, Bou Bekr Amhousha, who was known as the false prophet, *dajjal,* the Berber tribes defeated the army of Mawlay Sliman (1785-1829) and descended on the city of Meknes. There, the tribal leaders, along with some shurfa installed a sultan of their own, Ibrahim ben Yazid. Among the lay leaders of the movement was Hassan ben Hmmou ou Aziz, of the Ait Ndhir.[10]

Mawlay Abd Al-Rahman became Sultan in 1829. The Ait Ndhir appear then to have been nominally in submission to the makhzan. They were divided into three administrative units, each responsible to a qaid: M'mma Boubidmani, Hammou ould Jibli, and Sidi ben Naçer Aziz. The tribe also agreed to supply the Sultan with a contingent of warriors to aid him in his jihad against the Christians. Abd Al-Rahman was succeeded by Sidi Mohammad (1859-1875). The tribe was by then more or less localized on the southern edge of the Sais plain and the adjacent plateau. Al-Nasiri mentions one supreme qaid for the whole tribe: Al-Jibli of Ait Ouallal. However, internal autonomy was maintained.

The Ait Ndhir and Mawlay Hassan

The remembered history of the Ait Ndhir begins with the reign of the Sultan Mawlay Hassan (1875-1894) whose rule marked a brief period of florescence of the Alawi dynasty. In their accounts of recent tribal history, informants dated things by the various trips of the Sultan through their territory. To him also they attribute the final makeup and territorial distribution of the different tribal segments. Older tribesmen claim that they remember the Sultan and recount the stories that their fathers told them about the great Mawlay Hassan, who is always mentioned with awe and admiration despite the fact that "he was really an enemy of our people since he continually was trying to put an end to us as a tribe." This am-

---

[10]The whole affair of "La Revolte Berbère" is reminiscent of the crisis of 1911-1912 when the tribes came close to deposing the Alawis. Drague (1951:89) saw in the revolt a maraboutic reaction against the tentative Wahabism of Sultan Mawlay Sliman and his attempt to suppress the powers and privileges of the shurfa and marabouts. For the expedition of Mawlay Sliman against the Ait Ndhir, see Al-Zayyani (1967:75).

bivalent attitude of the Ndhiris toward sultans was typical. They held a personal respect and admiration for those sultans known for their fairness, justice, and power, at the same time that they opposed their political rule. Needless to say, the two attitudes of political rejection and affective recognition of and allegiance to the Sultan need not be exclusive; certainly they are not contradictory in the historical and psychic universe of Morocco. Part of the explanation lies in the shared attitudes toward the person of the Sultan in his capacity as a sharif.

It was ironical that the reign of Mawlay Hassan should coincide with a period of grave economic difficulties for Morocco. The completion of the Suez Canal in 1869 affected the established trade pattern in the Mediterranean by allowing the import to Europe of cheap raw materials from India and Australia, and the value of the raw products furnished until then by Morocco (wool, hides, and cereals) depreciated drastically. Steamships greatly facilitated intercontinental communication and Europe turned its commercial face westward, and the Atlantic replaced the Mediterranean as the center of international trade routes. Moroccan ports, never well kept up, deteriorated rapidly. By 1880, a sharp deficit in Morocco's commercial balance was evident. The country's imports far outstripped its exports and the situation was exacerbated by the heavy war indemnity that Morocco was paying to Spain following the loss of Tetouan in 1860. The customs revenues fell by 70 percent, causing the makhzan to bear down heavily on the tribes for revenue in the form of taxation. The Moroccan economist Ayache (1968) contends that it was the exorbitant war indemnity demanded by Spain that initiated the grave financial crisis that led in time to the establishment of the French Protectorate.

Between the years 1885 and 1894, yearly expeditions were sent to the Ait Ndhir and Beni Mguild territories with the object of collecting taxes. Sultan Hassan became known as "the sultan whose throne was the saddle." Al-Nasiri (1954-59:135-137) wrote that

> At the end of 1879, Mawley Hassan had to lead an army against the Beni Mtir whose reputation as highwaymen was known in all the region. The Sultan went to Agourai and El Hajeb and the Beni Mtir ran to the mountains.... However, the Sultan managed to encircle them near the forest of Afeqfaq [near Ifran]. The army had meanwhile pillaged their harvest and confiscated their grain. So they came to the Sultan and asked for his compassion, *shafa'a*. He lifted the siege after they promised him 500 men as hostages, *marhoun*, and agreed to pay 150,000 ryals. The Sultan then allowed them to go back to their traditional occupation of patrolling the Fez-Meknes road.

The Sultan also deported their war leader, Al-Jibli, to Marrakesh and divided the command of the tribe among eight qaids. One informant said, "Mawlay Hassan was a real Sultan. He really tried to put an end to us as a tribe; he used to gather our leaders and put them in jail. He and his army would come into our territory, but he was too poor and could not maintain large garrisons in the qasba, and as soon as his army left, we refused to pay the taxes."

At the death of Sultan Hassan in 1894, the tribe reverted to active dissidence, the appointed qaids were ignored, and the taxes were not sent to the treasury. The regent Ba Ahmad ruled for the young Sultan Abd Al-Aziz, and the Ait Ndhir were left on their own. Three qaids were nominally in command of the whole tribe but real authority went back to the "big tents."[11]

THE AIT NDHIR AT THE BEGINNING OF THE TWENTIETH CENTURY

Mawlay Hassan's favorite son, Abd Al-Aziz, was not the best sultan for the times. Affable and weak-willed, he was hardly capable of dealing with the political and financial chaos that was Morocco at the turn of the century. His court at Fez was a center for the intrigue of the various agents of the European governments and commercial firms that were competing for concessions and commitments to all kinds of political and economic privileges. Word of the "moral corruption" of the Sultan and his enthusiasm for, and manipulation by, the infidels soon spread all over the country. Harrassed by the French expansion in the west and south and uncertain of the ability of the makhzan to ward it off, the whole country broke into open rebellion. Routes between the coast and the inerior were no longer safe and the traditional makhzan triangle between the cities of Rabat, Meknes, and Fez was in revolt. The Ait Ndhir spilled farther onto the Sais and on at least one occasion attempted to pillage the markets at the city of Meknes. But the governor managed to close the city gates in time and avert the assault. The Ait Ndhir then had to make do with robbing caravans. The Sultan's policy, if it may be called that, alternated between sending an expedition to chastise the tribe and collect the overdue tax, a nominal one since it amounted to 1½ ryals per tent, and dispatching a Wazzani sharif who would talk them into good behavior. In around 1900, the Sultan named three qaids for the tribe and these were still in command when the French arrived.

To insure the security of their Algerian colony, the French

---

[11] Air Ndhir use the expression "big tent," Berber *takhamt takhatart*, when they refer to a powerful leader, a wealthy notable or a respected elder.

embarked on a series of campaigns that extended from south of Oran all the way across the Algerian border to the Moulouya river. Marshall Lyautey was in charge of the military operations that resulted in the occupation of Colomb-Bechar (1903), Bergent (1904), Oujda (1907), and Bou-Denib (1908). The Moroccan court was then in Marrakesh and the *Blad al Makhzan* was slowly reduced to the cities of Marrakesh and Fez and their immediate environs.

Everywhere, an atmosphere of fear and restlessness prevailed, heightened by the news of the steady French encroachment. Count Segonzac, who visited the Ait Ndhir region in 1901, wrote that the tribe was actually independent and practicing banditry. "The Beni Mtir are known for their brutality. When we reached their area, a group of their cavalry came out to greet us with guns, less a deputation to greet a *sharif* (Segonzac was travelling in the company of a *sharif* for protection) than a party out to kidnap. They came out in small formations, saluted and galloped away. Their horses were small but well handled" (1903:98; see also 106-112).

Sultan Abd Al-Aziz embarked on a series of administrative reforms and internal improvements that served to further alienate the tribesmen. In 1901, construction was begun on a railroad and telegraph system which was to connect Fez and Meknes, and eventually extend to the coast. The activity at the edge of their territory provoked fright among the Ait Ndhir, who suspected that the enterprise would interfere with the grazing movements of their flocks. In the fall of 1902, Abd Al-Aziz moved his court from Marrakesh to Fez. Soon afterward he introduced a series of tax reforms known as the *tartib*.[12] Modeled after the British income tax, the tartib was designed to replace the customary Quranic taxes with a fixed tax on all property. This tax was to apply equally to all the citizens, including the traditionally tax exempt shurfa and guish tribes. A series of revolts broke out among the guish; profiting from the confused circumstances, the Ait Ndhir increased their raiding activities, coming close to the walls of Fez and Meknes. Communications with the coast became precarious and the court in Fez was virtually in a state of seige.

Several pretenders made their appearance in the Moroccan countryside. The most famous of these was Bou Hmara who claimed to be the precursor of the Mahdi, and decried the "Christian ways" of the Sultan.[13] To meet this challenge, Abd Al-Aziz had to abandon

---

[12] For information on the nature of this tax and reaction to it, see G. Salmon, (1905:154-158) and E. Aubin (1904:254-456).

[13] For an account of Bou Hmara's rebellion, see E. Aubin (1904:108-131); Also L. Arnaud (1952:153-214).

all of his reform projects, and concentrate on stemming the tide of revolt.

For the next few years (until 1907) the Ait Ndhir remained relatively docile as they watched the fast changing political scene. One of the most significant developments was the rise of the influence of an Idrissi sharif,[14] Sidi Mohammad ben Abdel Kabir Al-Kettani. Al-Kettani was the respected leader of the Kettaniya brotherhood which was based in the city of Fez. Under his guidance the brotherhood attracted a large following among the elite of the city and among the Berber tribes nearby. Among the Ait Ndhir, it struck root only among the two clans of the Ait Harzallah and Ait Iqedarren.

Beginning in 1904, Al-Kettani emerged as the leader of the opposition to the French influence on the makhzan; he soon became a vocal and rabid critic of the Alawi Sultan's "collusion" with the infidels. His followers preached the necessity of a holy war. It must be mentioned that the Idrissi *shurfa*,[14] of whom Kettani was one, trace their descent to Mawlay Idriss, the most venerated of the Moroccan saints and the founder of the first Islamic dynasty in Morocco. The Idrissis therefore constitute a potential threat to the Alawi shurfa, since they too could provide the needed "legitimacy" for the sultanate.[15]

French Pacification and the Tribe

The French landed at Casablanca in August, 1907, following an uprising of the city's population against the European residents. Military activities were soon extended to the environs of the city among the Shawiya tribes. The reaction to this new invasion was swift. In Marrakesh, the Sultan's deputy (*khalifa*) was his brother, Abd Al-Hafiz who had been ruling the city for several years in virtual independence of Fez with the backing of the powerful Berber qaids of the western Anti Atlas. At the news of the invasion of Casablanca, and motivated no doubt by the prospect of forming their own makhzan, the qaids convinced Al-Hafiz to assume the sultanate in view of his brother's ineptitude. The 'ulemas of Marrakesh were soon won over and Mawlay Hafiz was declared the new sultan who was to lead the jihad against the infidels and save the country. In 1908, the royal cortege journeyed from Marrakesh to

---

[14]The different shurfa families in Morocco are grouped into two major branches: the Idrissis of Fez and the Alawis of Tafilalet.

[15]On the threat of the Idrissi to the Alawis, see E. Michaux-Bellaire (1914:393-395).

Fez following the inland "Berber Route" (Tadla, Khenifra, Amros). The Berber tribes en route received the new Sultan with gifts and declarations of allegiance. He lingered long enough among the powerful Zayan tribe to marry a daughter of the "Zayani King," Moha ou Hammou. Afterwards he was escorted by the Ait Ndhir as he made his way through their territory to Fez. His brother, Mawlay Abd Al-Aziz, had meanwhile fled the capital, and a delegation of that city's notables and 'ulema, including Sidi Al-Kettani himself, came out to receive him and to declare their allegiance. But the new Sultan's inability to stem the tide of rebellion and general anarchy, and his manifest collaboration with the French, soon shook the confidence of all those who had expected a radical change under his leadership. As one informant put it, "Hafiz was khalifa in Marrakesh. Then the Glaouis and Mtouggis convinced him to become a sultan *mujahid* [that is to say, one who will lead the holy war]. The Zayan[16] received him with gifts and told us to do likewise. Our shurfa said that Hafiz was a good man and a good Moslem and that he would lead a jihad to free our country. So we supported him. But after he got to Fez, he became only a sultan and not a mujahid."

In March of 1909, Sidi Al-Kettani fled Fez and took refuge among the Ait Ndhir. A clan of the tribe, the Ait Harzallah, granted him their protection and some claim that he married a tribeswoman who bore him a son. Mawlay Al-Hafiz ordered the tribe to hand over the refugee and, as Al-Kettani was preparing to leave for Beni Mguild territory, he was betrayed by several Ait Ndhiri notables. He was arrested and taken as a prisoner to Fez where he was put to death. The elders of the tribe are very ambivalent about the "Kettani incident" and are reluctant to discuss it. French historians claim that Al-Kettani was actively raising contingents among the Ait Ndhir to fight the Sultan. The Ndhiris deny this and claim that they gave him their protection because he was an important sharif and that they were not aiding an Idrissi usurper. Be that as it may, the betrayal of a holy sharif by tribal members on their own territory brought shame and fear to the tribe. An old informant from the Ait Harzallah said, "As the *makhzan 'askar* (soldiers) came close to the sharif, one of them hit him with the end of the rifle. The sharif then turned his head and as he was being led away said in a loud voice, 'Oh Beni Mtir, I have left you the fire that can never be

---

[16] The Zayan were a powerful Berber confederation to the west of the Ait Ndhir. At the time they were ruled tyranically by a feudal leader, Moha ou Hammou, from his fortress in Khenifra. The Ait Ndhir were hardly in a position to defy the Zayan and to expose their western flank to reprisals.

quenched ('Ya Beni Mtir khaletulkum l'afya lmateqdash') and his curse was soon fulfilled for before long the French were upon us and 'ate'[17] us up. They took our land, our freedom, and made us work the corvée."

Partly to punish them for their support of Al-Kettani and partly to impose general order, the Sultan sent a military column, *maḥalla*, against the Ait Ndhir. It was defeated near El Hajeb and tribesmen claim that part of the army defected to their side. In May, another column led by General M. LeGlay, containing contingents from the Haouz of Marrakesh and French artillery officers, defeated the Ait Ndhir and occupied the qasba of El Hajeb. The tribe was then fighting under the command of three war leaders: Hammou ou Lahcen, Bougrine Al-Arj, and Bou Azz Al-Moulwani. They were made to pay a heavy war indemnity and to furnish 300 men for the army. Several tribal notables were taken as hostages to Fez.

During the years 1909-1911, the tribe was relatively peaceful under the command of two leaders, Mahjoubi Al-Bourzouine and Miloudi. In 1910, the Sultan gave the region as a tax farm to Madani Al-Glawi, the famous feudal lord of the High Atlas. Al-Glawi proceeded to send his armies to the area to extract the taxes from the tribesmen. In 1911, the tribe rebelled under the leadership of 'Aqqa Al-Boubidmani and Mokhtar Al-Hammadi. This rebellion coincided with the revolt of the Oudaya, a guish tribe near Fez.[18] The Oudaya were protesting the reorganization of the army by the French instructors. It is interesting that such French historians as André Martin subsume all of the different tribal rebellions under the general rubric of "guerre sainte," thus stressing the xenophobic reaction of the Moslem tribes to Christians. Tribesmen themselves do not utilize the jihad idiom at this juncture of their history and point to the extortion in taxes, conscription, and corvée as the concrete causes for their dissent. No doubt, there was xenophobia and general apprehension of the naṣara, but to categorize the reaction at the time simply as religious hostility serves to distort reality and to falsify history.

On April 27, 'Aqqa Al-Boubidmani, rebel leader of the Ait Ndhir, Gerwan, and the Zemmour, (to whom the French fancifully referred as "Le Sultan Berbère") declared Mawlay Zein, a brother of Mawlay Al-Hafiz, then living in Meknes, the new sultan of Mo-

---

[17] The expression "ate" is used by Moroccans to mean conquer, devastate, destroy.

[18] On a possible conspiracy among the tribes, see Henri Gaillard, "L'insurrection des tribue de la region de Fez," *Rensignement Coloniaux*, 1911.

rocco. The 'ulema of the nearby shrine of Sidi Idriss Al-Zerhoun confirmed his selection. He was given a skeletal cabinet that included several Berber notables. But the coup was short-lived for the French immediately dispatched a large army from Fez. The rebels were defeated and both Mawlay Zein and 'Aqqa Al-Boubidmani surrendered to General Moinier. Following this, a group of Ait Ndhir elders surrendered and accompanied a French column to El Hajeb. However, several other notables of the tribe refused to surrender and left, accompanied by their families and animals to join the dissident Mguild and Seghrouchen. The three leaders of the dissident Ndhiris were Haddou n'Hmousha, Mammou ou Aziz, and Moha ou Rahu.

Those of the tribe who were nominally pacified soon started to chafe under the weight of the heavy taxes and the war indemnity being collected by the French in the name of the makhzan. A delegation of tribal notables went to Fez and demanded an audience with the Ntouggi, the minister of reclamations. They asked for a reprieve from taxation; but none was forthcoming. With the French at the helm, the tax collection was more efficient than ever.[19] The Army confiscated the tribe's animals and crops for tax reparations. In February and well before the period of transhumance, the French officers noted with alarm that many Ait Ndhiri were leaving the plain area for the mountains. In April of that year, the Sultan's troops mutinied against their French officers and almost simultaneously the surrounding tribes went into rebellion and descended on the walls of Fez. An Idrissi sharif and holy man, *marabout*, Sidi Rahu Al-Seghrouchni emerged as the rallying leader of all the dissident Berber elements in the eastern part of the region. By now, the Ait Ndhiri were hopelessly split. Army intelligence estimated that out of a total of 1,700 tents, 800 were in dissidence. Of those who capitulated, 450 were put under command of Driss ou Raho near Bou Semsel and the rest were under the command of Djilali ou Alla near Qasba Arroub. However, the French garrisons in the field were underequipped and were unable to protect the Ait Ndhir who were being raided by their still rebellious cousins.

The rebel tribesmen fought a fast, guerilla style war. A group of cavalry would descend and cut the telegraph lines or ambush a supply column and then retreat into the mountains. The failure of the stationary French garrisons to repulse these attacks increased the audacity of the tribesmen who raided as far onto the plain as Bou Fekrane. The rebel leaders, Sidi Rahu, Ali n'Hmoucha, and Moha ou Neba of the Mguild, attempted to coordinate the war effort and

---

[19] The Treaty of the Protectorate was signed on March 30, 1912 at Fez.

assaults were launched simultaneously on Fez, Sefrou, and El Hajeb. The Ait Ndhir remember this supra-tribal cooperation as a unique and extraordinary event in their history. LeGlay (1918) speculated that had there been more organization and coordination among the tribes, it would certainly have spelled the end of the Alawi dynasty.

No More Dissidence, The Ait Ndhir Pacified

In January of 1913, the western Ait Ndhir (Ait Bourzouine) rebelled under their new war leader, Hammou ou Lahcen. They left the plain for the plateau and joined sections of the dissident Gerwan. To stem this new development in the western part of the region, a column of French soldiers was quickly dispatched from El Hajeb. The soldiers were attacked while still en route by a combined cavalry force made up of the Ait Ndhir and the Beni Mguild. The column was forced to retreat to the qasba of El Hajeb. Confident of their own power, the tribes began to prepare an offensive south of Agourai and did in fact attack El Hajeb. On March 19, contingents of the Zemmour, Ait Ndhir, Gerwan, and Beni Mguild came close to the walls of Meknes, causing general panic among the urban population.

Thoroughly alarmed by now, the French proceeded to reorganize the lines of command in the area. A "Cèrcle des Ait Ndhir" was created and placed under the direct command of Colonel Henrys, a veteran of the south Algerian campaigns. Marshall Lyautey's directives were very clear: to pacify all of the Ait Ndhir simultaneously along with the Gerwan and the Sais Arabs. Force was to be used to establish influence and to inspire fear and respect while at the same time "political education" was to be applied to establish friendly contact and win the confidence of the tribal notables. The task force assigned to the Cèrcle included four battalions, two squadrons, two batteries, and one-half of a company. Taking the offensive and using mobile convergent columns with heavy cannons, Colonel Henrys managed to dismember the Berber bloc and to subdue it piecemeal. The Ait Ndhir who were in the mountains were faced with the possibility of losing their lowlands permanently and of having to remain among the Beni Mguild and the Seghrouchen. Always pragmatic in war, they decided to surrender. By 1914, the last remnants of resistance among the Ait Ndhir were overcome and the tribe joined the roster of "les tribus Marocaines soumis." As one old informant put it, "the Sultan had found himself a new guish tribe . . . a very powerful one that came and stayed." He was referring to the French Army. There is no doubt that the resistance of the Ait Ndhir to French pacification was motivated, at least partially, by their conviction that the French Army came to impose the rule of the makhzan.

The French had by now occupied what Marshall Lyautey called "Le Maroc utile," but they still had to conquer what General LeGlay referred to as "Le Maroc indispensable." The "Maroc utile" roughly was equivalent to the traditional *bled al makhzan*. At this juncture of their Moroccan adventure and with World War I threatening, the French cabinet discussed the possibility of holding onto only the plains and letting the mountains go. But Marshall Lyautey pointed out that "if we do not occupy the mountains, the mountains will occupy us." And Bugeaud added that "il faut être maître partout, sous peine de n'être en securité nulle part." Thus the French proceeded to save the throne of the Alawi shurfa and stayed long enough to erect a modern nation on the ruins of a decayed makhzan.

III

ECOLOGY AND TRADITIONAL ECONOMIC ORGANIZATION

THE Ait Ndhir were a transhumant tribe inhabiting the foothills of the Middle Atlas and the neighboring plains as far as the city of Meknes. Today they are predominantly a sedentary people, although some clans, notably the Ait Harzallah, still practice limited transhumance. The Ait Ndhir occupied a special ecological niche in a politically, socially, and geographically transitional area of Morocco. This chapter describes the traditional economic adaptation of the tribe to the territory which they occupied between 1860 and 1912. The area was essentially a zone of passage within the larger, geographically transitional, Meknes region.

THE ECOLOGICAL SETTING

What appears on the maps as the Middle Atlas mountain chain is actually a highly complex region made up of different zones with great variation, both in altitude and in annual precipitation (see Figs. 3 and 4). The two major parts of the Middle Atlas consist of an extended plateau and a mountain chain. The plateau rises gradually, beginning at Fez (altitude: 387 meters) and ending in the Guigou valley (altitude: 1300 meters). The plateau is actually divided into two sections separated by a sharp and sudden rise in elevation which extends as a sharp escarpment from the town of El Hajeb to that of Sefrou. The northern and lower part of the plateau is considered part of the Sais plain, itself a broad, sloping area approximately 50 miles in length and 20 miles in width; its stretches of flat land are intermingled with low rolling hills. Lying on the northern edge of the mountain belt, the Sais plain forms one of Morocco's most favored rainfall areas, receiving an average annual precipitation of 600-700 millimeters (Comité de Geographie du Maroc: Atlas du Maroc, Planche No. 4a). The Sais lies 400 feet above sea level on its western end and 1600 feet above sea level on

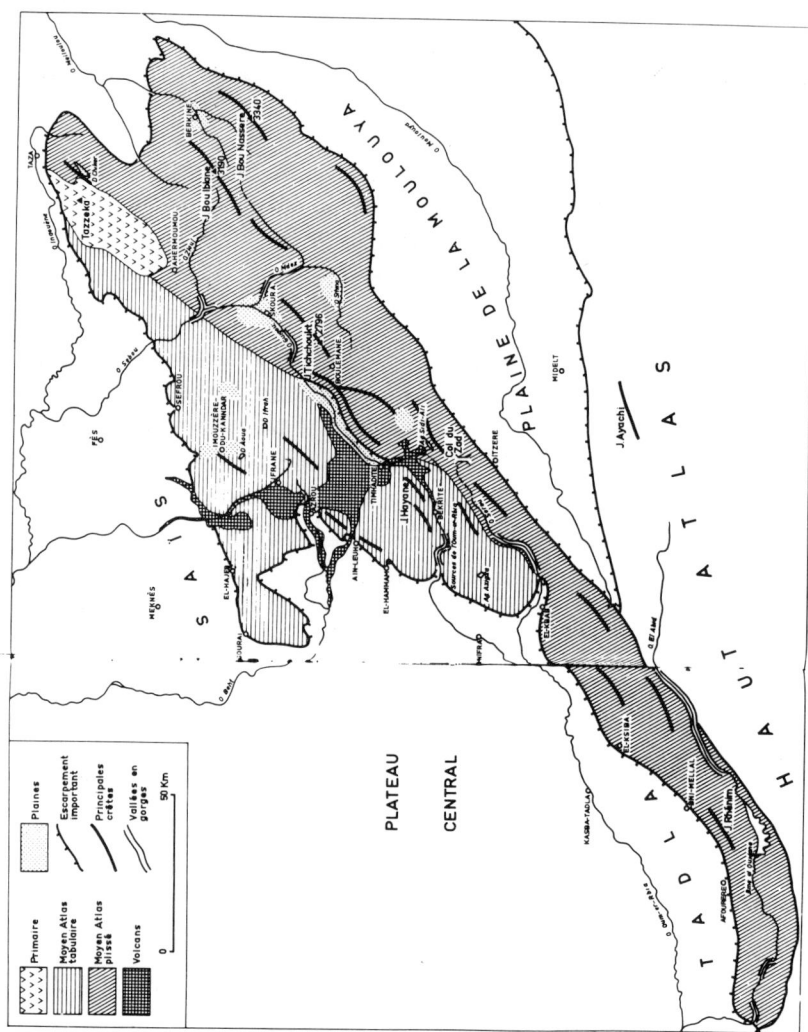

Fig. 3. Relief map of the Middle Atlas (from *Geographie du Maroc*, pp. 116-117).

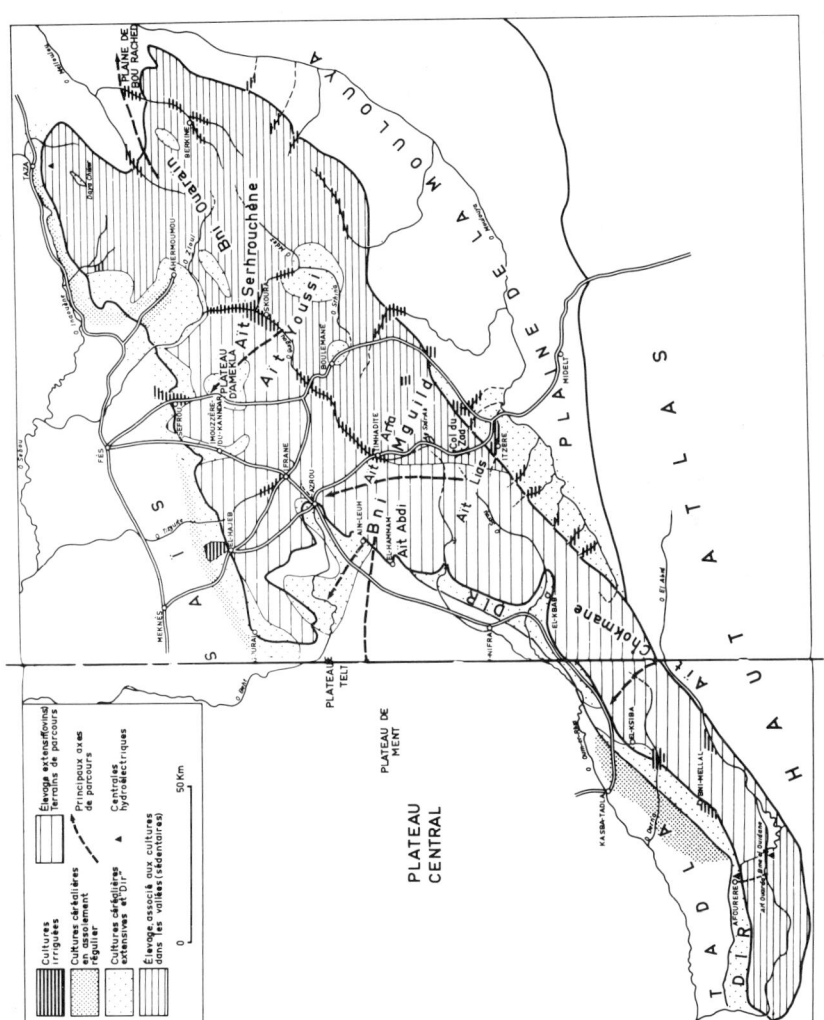

Fig. 4. Economy of the Middle Atlas (from *Geographie du Maroc*, pp. 124-125).

its eastern and drier edge.[1] The region of the plain that joins the foothills of the Middle Atlas is known to the natives as the *dir*, or slope. It is a well watered region, forested and covered with lush pasture throughout the dry and hot summer months.

Politically, the dir formed the contact and friction zone between the makhzan-dominated plains and the Tamazight-speaking populations of the Middle Atlas. In general, the Berbers remained throughout history the masters of the dir and of the mountains behind it. But it took very aggressive tribes to gain and to sustain a foothold on the plain, while, at the same time, holding onto their pastures in the higher adjacent plateau. Those who succeeded managed to pursue a mixed economy, combining limited agriculture (mainly cereals) with extensive pastoralism. Such dir tribes as the Zayan, the Gerwan, and the Ait Ndhir had a widespread reputation for being cruel and warlike, a reputation they no doubt encouraged. Segonzac (1903:98) wrote that he was warned against travelling among the Ait Ndhir, despite the fact that he was accompanied throughout his journey by one of the most venerated shurfa in the region. He wrote that after spending the night at some village on the Sais: "nous entrons ce matin en pays Braber, dans la tribu des Beni Mtir. Le paysage reste a peu près le même; ces gens changent de type, de moeurs et de langue. Une escorte est venue nous quéris, fusil au poing. Le trait caracteristique de ces Berbèrs est la brutalité. En venant à la recontre du chérif, ils entendent lui rendre homage sans doute, mais leur visite semble plutôt une prise de possèssion, un enlèvement."

It was to guard against the further encroachment of the dir tribes that Moroccan sultans installed several guish tribes in a safety belt fashion around the two cities of the Sais: Fez and Meknes.[2] Fez is considered to be the Islamic bourgeois city par excellence. Founded in 808 by Mawlay Idriss, Fez has a long history as a leading center for Islamic learning, centered around the famous university of Al-Qarawiyin. As the leading commercial and craft center of Morocco, it developed a large and wealthy class of merchants and craftsmen. It is still the repository of the Moroccan Arab ethos and the style setter for the traditionally oriented urban bourgeoisie. Meknes was founded in the tenth century and named after the Zenata of Meknasa, an Arabic-speaking tribe that came from the

---

[1] Early in the Protectorate, the French discovered that the Sais was high enough, yet frost free, for the dormant period of grapevines. The region soon became the center of viniculture and the site of massive land appropriation.

[2] Fez is the larger city with a population of 216,133 in 1960, compared to 175,943 for Meknes.

ECOLOGY AND TRADITIONAL ECONOMIC ORGANIZATION 39

east and settled in the area. The city enjoyed its greatest fame during the reign of the second Alawi Sultan, Mawlay Ismail (1672-1727). The Sultan made it his capital and used it as the base from which he embarked on a series of conquests to enlarge and consolidate his empire. Since that time, and despite certain commercial and handicraft activities, Meknes has declined in importance.

Following the establishment of the Protectorate, French administrators and military personnel moved into Meknes and by the 1950s it had become a busy regional capital for the modern agricultural region around it. However, it is still considered a parvenue, lacking a true style of its own. It is interesting to note that the Ndhiris today combine a general hatred of the inhabitants of Fez (Fassis) with a grudging admiration and envy of their style of life. Well-to-do tribesmen seek to imitate the manners and customs of the city, while at the same time being very conscious of their own cultural and ethnic marginality. The inhabitants of Fez, in their turn, consider all non-Fassis in general as uncultured and the rural Berber as savage.

THE TRIBAL TERRITORY

The territory occupied by the Ait Ndhir at the time of their submission to the French consisted of an approximate total of 150,000 hectares. Out of this total, only one-third was on the plain proper, the bulk of the territory or 100,000 hectares was composed of mountains: the plateaus of El Hajeb and Ifran and the intervening stony plain of Sidi 'Issa. In 1914, the French estimated that the tribe had farmed about half of their land on the plain. This stretched between the first plateau and the Fez-Meknes road.[3]

The most remarkable topographical feature of the tribal territory is the sudden sharp drop in altitude (200 meters), known as the cliff of El Hajeb.[4] This drop forms a continuous escarpment that neatly divides the tribal area into two ecological zones: the plain to the northwest and the plateau to the southwest. The plain is exceptionally fertile and well-watered. In addition to its abundant rainfall, it benefits from the many streams and springs that come down from the foothills. The plateau, however, is rocky and with the exception of a few scattered depressions, is generally unsuitable

---

[3] Information comes from the war records at Vincennes.

[4] El Hajeb is still considered an Ait Ndhir town. In 1960, it had a population of 8,000 people.

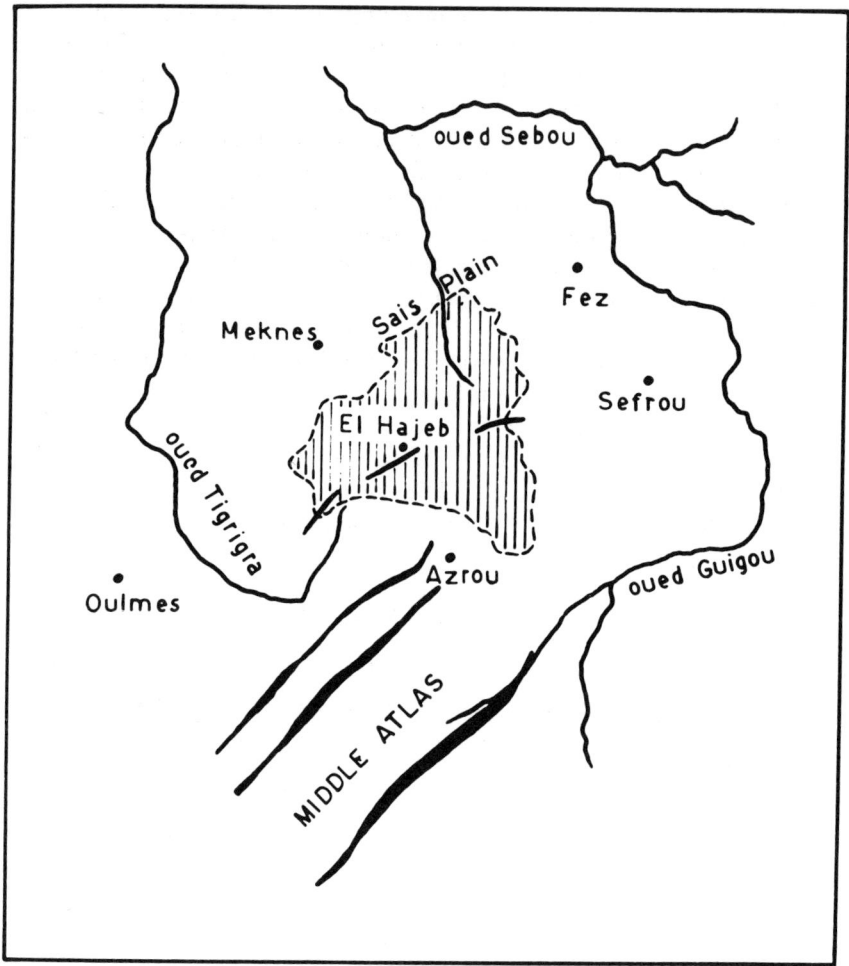

Fig. 5. Sketch map of the territory of the Ait Ndhir.

for agriculture. Thus, the plain and the plateau complement one another, offering a unique combination of abundant fertile agricultural land with good, high altitude summer pastures. The Ait Ndhir exploited this combination in their seasonal migrations.

The tribal territory has no natural frontiers, and the Ait Ndhir define their boundaries in terms of the groups with whom they come in contact. Thus they will say "our territory, *tamazirit-n-nun*, stretched in the west to the Gerwan and Zayan, to the north to

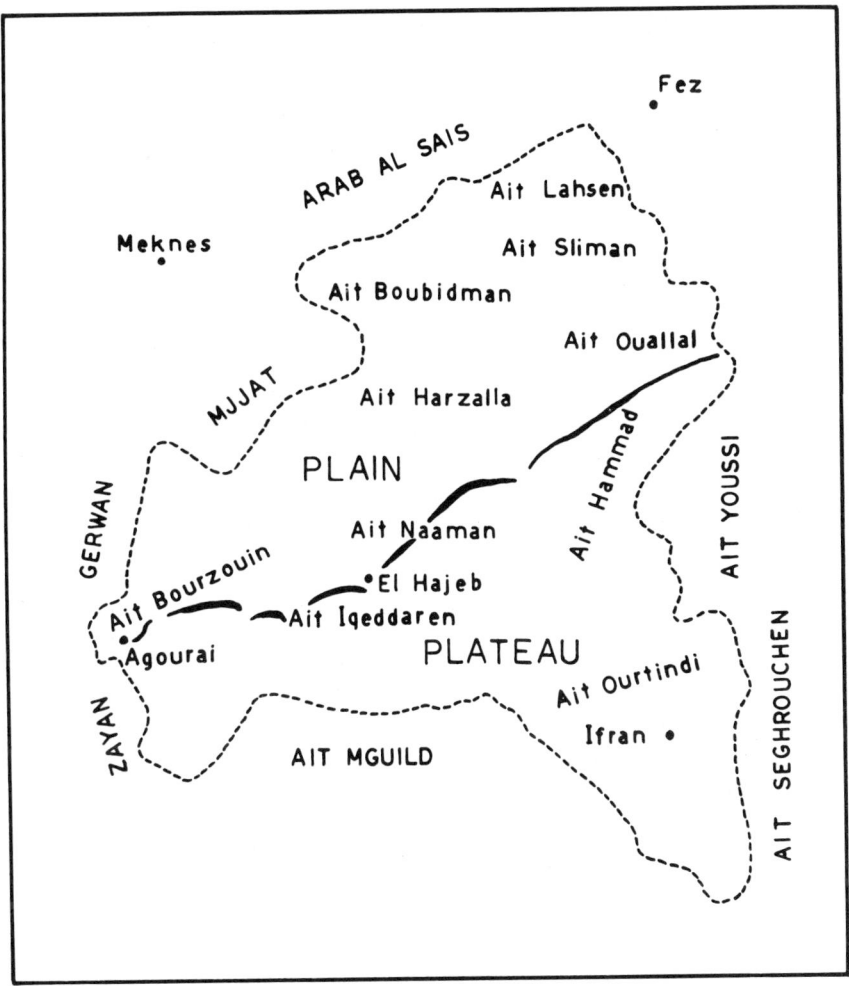

Fig. 6. Sketch map of the Ait Ndhir territory showing the distribution of the clans. ⌒ = Cliffs separating the plains from the high plateau area.

Arab al Sais and the Mjjat to the south until the Beni Mguild and to the east until you get to the Youssi and Seghrouchen." In geographical terms, this means that their northern limit is the Meknes-Fez road,[5] to the east Oued Nja and the plateau of Reba'a, to the south their area extended to Sidi 'Issa al Fras, and to the west to the qasba of Agourai.

---

[5] When the tribe was not in rebellion, sultans would officially entrust the Ait Ndhir with patrolling the Fez-Meknes road.

TRADITIONAL ECONOMY OF THE AIT NDHIR

Early travellers to the area (Foucould, Rohlfs, Segonzac) agree that the tribe was predominantly pastoral. They were described as nomadic, living in tents and possessing large flocks of sheep. Walter Harris, a correspondent for the London *Times* (and an agent for his government), visited the area in 1897 and wrote:

> ... this recent journey was to a district lying south of a line drawn from Fes through Meknes.... This region may be roughly described as Central Morocco. Five large and important tribes inhabit this region. Two others (Ait Tsgaruchen and Ait Youssi) are by the natives included in this group.... These are all nomadic. The five tribes to be considered are, then, Zimmur, Geruan, Zaian, Beni Mtir and Beni Mguild. Owing to their nomadic habits, it is impossible to place them upon one map, for a country which is filled with the Beni Mguild in winter becomes in summer the resort of all the other tribes.... [All of these tribes] are entirely dwellers in tents, and, for the most part, nomadic. The Beni Mguild have, it is true, built some villages on the higher peaks of the Atlas, but these are only inhabited in summer, and are entirely deserted as soon as the snow commences, when the inhabitants seek the lower and more clement districts with their tents. It will thus be seen that this large tract of land—over 100 miles in length and averaging some 50 in breadth—is almost devoid of any buildings, such as there are being entirely "ksors" or fortresses, erected at various times by the Moorish sultans in their attempts to enforce their authority upon the people. A glance at the two sketch maps [see Fig. 8] appended will show the respective positions of the tribes in summer and winter.... It will be seen from the maps that the two tribes of Zimmur and Geruan make but a slight movement to the south, the Beni Mtir and Zaian sharing most of the region in which they become in spring and summer neighbors, to be separated again in the autumn and winter by the Beni Mguild.... The Berbers all pitch their tents in circles, the tents being of goat's hair dyed a very dark shade of purple, almost black, with the rinds and husks of pomegranate. Into the circle are driven the flocks and herds of cattle at night time, and the entrance, a space left between two tents, is closed by a hurdle of thorns.... The principal occupation of the Berber tribes is the tending of flocks and herds, there being but little cultivation. On the plain south of Meknes and Fes, a rich, dark, loamy soil appears here and there, and is ploughed during the winter. Some of the areas near the ouds produce good crops of wheat and barley. But the Berber is essentially a shepherd, and it is for the grazing of his flocks and herds that he spends the summer in wandering from spot to spot in the forest. The Beni Mtir, who spend their winter in the northern plain, return to the forest ... and do not return until it is time to reap the grain which they have sown in winter (Harris, 1897:642-644).

The Ait Ndhir admit today that they were really a pastoral people who disliked agriculture but had to do it "so that we might

ECOLOGY AND TRADITIONAL ECONOMIC ORGANIZATION 43

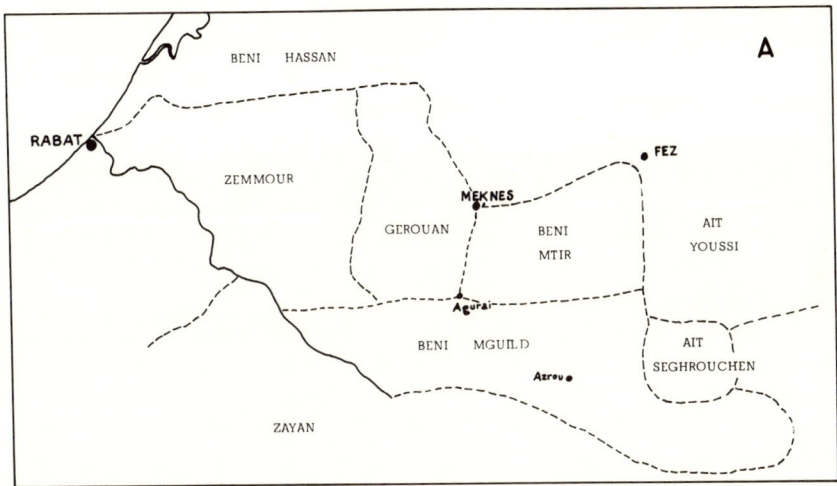

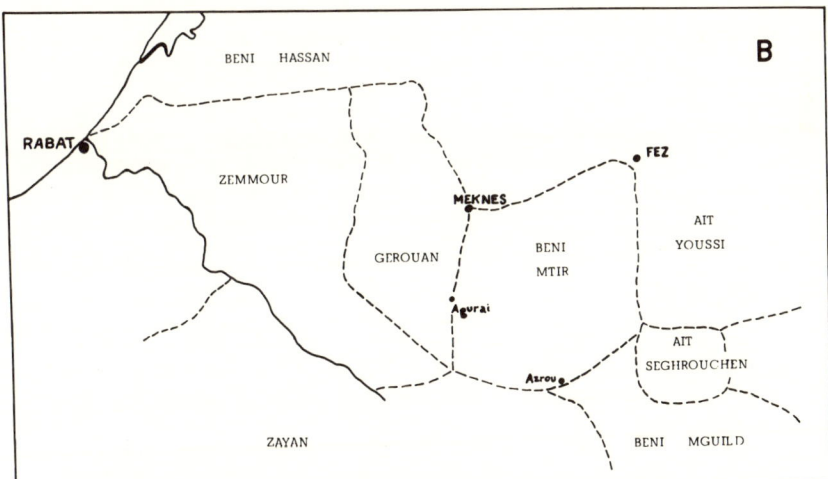

Fig. 7. Sketch map showing the relative positions of the five nomadic tribes: a. before the annual spring migration; b. after the annual spring migration (from Harris, 1897).

eat."[6] Unlike their neighbors, the Beni Mguild, the Ndhiris had no permanent houses on their winter grounds. Prior to the arrival of the French in the area, there were only a handful of houses and these belonged to shurfa and qaids who lived amidst their 'azibs.[7] The only "villages" were the two qasbas of El Hajeb and Agourai. El Hajeb was a fortified complex built by Mawley Hassan on the slope overlooking the plains. It was intended to house sharifian troops left by the Sultan to keep an eye on the Ait Ndhir. In time, the troops deserted because of lack of pay and the qasba became the site of a weekly souq (market) for the tribe. The army headquarters were converted into a hostelry for the itinerant Jewish and Arab merchants who came from Fez and travelled the area under the *mezraq (amur)* protection.

The qasba of Agourai was built by Mawlay Ismail (1722-1757) and is located 18 miles south of Meknes. Local tradition has it that the qasba was built to accommodate the Christian slaves and renegades who fell into the hands of the Sultan in his wars against the Portuguese and the Spanish. Certainly many of the surnames in the town today give some credibility to the story, for among these are found names such as Al-Gitano and Al-Espanioli. Furthermore, the inhabitants of the town are collectively referred to as "awlad Al-'Alouj," *'Alouj*, plural of *'ilj*, is an Arabic word meaning "infidel, lout, uncouth."

Agourai itself served as a site for another of the rural souqs in the area. The following selection from Harris' account serves to illustrate the anarchy and general condition of insecurity that prevailed in the area at the turn of the present century, as well as the important role that these rural markets played in the economic life of the tribesmen.

> Although the tribes enumerated above [Gerwan, Ait Ndhir and Beni Mguild] came from one stock and are closely allied, forming a distinct branch of the Berber race in Morocco, it must by no means be thought that they live at peace among themselves. Every tribe, and often the subdivisions of tribes, is at war with its neighbors, and at the "sok", or market, outside Agurai, which all patronize, so common has become bloodshed and murder, that today only the members of one tribe market

---

[6]The reputation of the Ndhiris as poor farmers persisted under the French. Colons in the area imported Riffis who were thought to be superior farm hands to the Ait Ndhir. Officials in the area always insisted that the tribe is still at heart a pastoral one despite all the sedentarization, adding that the Ait Ndhir's "primordial" disrespect for the land led to their massive loss of it. The story is not that simple.

[7]*'Azibs* were land concessions given by sultans to shurfa or qaids, usually on territory of submissive tribes. A more detailed account of this form of land tenure will be discussed further on.

at a time. As soon as they have completed their purchases or their sales, they mount their horses and ride away, leaving the scene free to another batch who have been waiting their departure and watching them from some hilltop nearby. The writer's presence at Agurai caused no little commotion among the people, for apparently no other traveller, at least in the memory of man, had preceded him and the members of the tribe of Beni Mguild, who were in the market at the time, one and all anxious to question the "Rumi", as they call a European, refused to go until the Zemouris, seated on a hilltop, sent a message to the writer, asking him to disappear for a while, so that the Beni Mgild might depart, and thus give them a chance of marketing (Harris, 1897:645).

The economic ties between the Ait Ndhir and the cities of Fez and Meknes seem to have been minimal despite the geographical proximity. Like most of the Middle Atlas tribes, the Ait Ndhir tended to be economically autarkic, living off the products of their animals and on the crops they planted. However, one must not minimize the importance of the itinerant merchants who traveled in the tribal territory and sold guns, ammunition, sugar, tea, and fabric. On the other hand, there are no records of any urban merchants holding debts of tribesmen, nor were there any outsiders who owned land within the tribal territory before the Protectorate.

THE SEASONAL MIGRATION

The Middle Atlas is the region of transhumance in Morocco. Tribal seasonal movements vary from one zone to another and from one year to the next (see Célérier, 1939:57-67). Some tribes, such as the Zayan and the Beni Mguild, cover great distances (average of 100 kilometers) between their summer and winter grounds and are, therefore, considered true nomads. During the period under consideration, the Ait Ndhir practiced limited transhumance, some clans travelling a distance of 30 kilometers but the majority travelling less.[8] Since they straddle the two zones of the plateau and the plain, the Ait Ndhir transhumance patterns rarely interconnect with those of neighboring tribes. In exceptionally dry summers, some Ait Ndhir clans would pasture in land which in winter was occupied by the Mguild or the Seghrouchen. In severe winter months, the process was reversed and tribes in the mountains would come down on the El Hajeb plateau.

It is impossible to reduce the nomadic movement of the tribe to any neat scheme. One could say that they summered in the high

---

[8] The Ait Ndhir differentiate between the two kinds of nomadism, calling the long distance type characteristic of the Mguild, *njou'*, and their own limited version, *rḥil*. Both words are Arabic: njou' means to seek a pasture, while rḥil simply means to migrate.

pastures on the plateaus and wintered on the plains where they planted their crops. In reality, even the simplest scheme must include anywhere from four to five stages and the calendar year is reduced in their eyes to the succession of these stages. Beginning in September, and throughout October, animals were sent down from the high pastures and were put out to eat the stubble from the harvest. In November, the rest of the animals and people followed and the general descent to the low ground was completed. By January, the douars[9] had regrouped in their proper areas on the plain and the tribe became several agglomerations of tents scattered over the territory.[10] Each large extended family was grouped into one sector, *rif*, separated by some distance from another such group. The tents were usually arranged in a circle facing inward, inside of which a wooden enclosure, *zriba*, was erected for the animals. Young men and shepherds took the sheep and goats out to pasture, leaving the cows near the douars. The women kept busy inside their tents, weaving the carpets, new tents, and the winter garments. There seems to have been very little interfamily cooperation in the douar; each household appeared to function independently. The only exception was the *tawellat*. *Tawellat* is the Tamazight noun from the Arabic verb *walla*: to put in charge. Under this arrangement, families that owned six cows or fewer would take turns rounding up the animals in the morning and putting them to pasture for that day. Those families with larger herds of cows were not eligible to join the tawellat; they had to hire their own shepherds or take care of the animals themselves. It should be added that the tawellat institution is still practiced among some of the Ndhiri douars.

In March preparations began for the ascent into the high areas; the larger tents were dismantled and packed away. If the tribe was not at war during that time, the women and children started the march, accompanied by only a few of the men. The majority of the adult males stayed behind to prepare the ground for spring cultivation. Each family usually cultivated the land immediately surrounding its tents. They would turn the soil over using simple ploughs, *ard*, and plant the seeds between the clumps of the palmetto (*doum*) that covered the area.[11] They planted legumes—beans,

---

[9] A douar is a common term in rural Morocco referring to any settlement. In the present context, it means a number of tents or a camp unit.

[10] For a discussion of the different settlement patterns and kinds of tents found in the Middle Atlas, see E. Laoust, 1930:151-153; 1932:115-218.

[11] Most of the wooden implements and utensils used by the Ait Ndhir were made by a shurfa group (Ait Sidi and Abd al Slamm) that lived near Ifran.

chick peas and lentils—occasionally adding a few such vegetables as tomatoes and cucumbers. The basic diet of the Ait Ndhir consisted of *ksou ksou* (couscous), flat bread, milk and its byproducts, and an occasional meat stew.

If the tribe was at war, or expected to be raided, a sufficient number of armed mounted men preceded the women and children in order to insure the security of the animals. By June, the people and animals would have reached the highest pastures and the tribe would be dispersed, the tents widely separated from one another. Men went down to the plain to harvest the wheat and barley; part of the crop was taken back for immediate consumption but the bulk was stored in underground bins called *mars* (Arabic *maṭamer*), along with collected honey and wool. During this time, men irrigated the sorghum and maize that constituted their summer crops. Trenches were dug across the fields and water fed into them from the oueds nearby. The sorghum and maize were not harvested till August or early September. Toward the end of September the animals started to descend and were put out to eat the stubble from the harvest. In October and before the rains started, men began to prepare the ground for the following year's fields. By November, everyone was down on the lowlands and the tents had regrouped in their original camp units.

Repeated questioning of the old men failed to reveal any image of a massive, well organized, rhythmic migration pattern of people and animals; instead a number of successive, small movements were described that differed in scale between the various clans and within the same clan from one year to the next. Some clans, such as the Ait Sliman and Ouallal, seemed to have travelled very little. Informants said that some families among the Ait Sliman used to send their animals to pasture in summer among the Ait Ourtindi, while they themselves stayed on the plain and concentrated on their farming. This trend toward sedentarization and increasing emphasis on cultivation among the Ait Sliman is confirmed by a report written in 1938. While discussing the problems of rural Morocco, A. Latron, a French agronomist, included an aerial photograph of the Meknes region with the comment that one could distinguish in the photograph "un partie de la fraction des Ait Slimane, on y distingue les habitations groupées, les jardins, les terres, partagée en longue bandes. Il y a là un hameau sedentarisé depuis assez longtemps et qui a resisté a notre expansion" (1938: 178).

Two segments of the Beni Mguild—Ait Irklaouen and Ait Arfa—sent part of their flocks each winter to pasture on Ndhir territory. In theory, the groups involved had a long standing agreement on the dues (in sheep) that the Beni Mguild had to pay in exchange for the use of the pasture. However, the practice can best be described in the words of a Ndhiri informant who said, "If we felt ourselves strong that year, then we demanded our rightful dues; but if we did not want to risk a fight, we forgot about the dues and allowed the i'zabben to come down anyway." The i'zabben referred to the shepherds who accompanied the flocks. The men, being without their families, dwelt in small, mobile tents called 'ziba. In 1921 the French officers in the field undertook the regulation of the transhumant movements in the region, both within and among the different tribes. With their usual Cartesian approach, they soon worked out a very neat pattern for the migration routes of the Mguild, Gerwan, and Ndhir. French officers, accompanied by the tribal qaids, supervised the yearly migrations and maintained order.

FORMS OF ECONOMIC COOPERATION

The relative economic autarky in which the Ndhiri lived, maintaining a precarious balance between extensive agriculture and animal husbandry, plus the absence of individual property in land, rendered a true class differentiation difficult to develop and maintain. Despite some differential in wealth, the Ait Ndhir seem to have constituted a relatively egalitarian society. Their recent installation in the area and their chronic political instability prevented any large scale accumulation of capital, measured solely in terms of sheep. Destitute members of the tribe were employed as shepherds, and in time they could start their own flocks. Strangers, usually men from the Rif or the Sahara, were employed as sharecroppers, *akhemmas*. Under the sharecropping system prevalent in all the Maghreb, the sharecropper supplied only his labor in return for one-fifth of the crop, hence the term *akhemmas*, "he who gets the fifth." Informants repeatedly said that all the sharecroppers among the Ait Ndhir were outsiders to the tribe, the majority being Arab al Sais.[12]

Large douars usually set a special tent aside to serve as their *timizgida*, or mosque. The jma'a hired a religious teacher, *ḍalb*, or *fqih*, to live in the tent-mosque. His duties consisted of leading the

---

[12] Arab al Sais refers to a number of Arab speaking tribal segments living near the city of Meknes. They were brought from the Algerian border and installed as guish tribes by the Sultan Mawlay Hassan in his effort to contain the rebellious Mjjat. The clans of Arab al Sais include Dkhissa, Mhaya, Douymania, and Weld Nsair. Abes (1918:65) mentions that in 1914, there were only a handful of sharecroppers (*akhemmasen*) among the Ait Ndhir.

prayers, teaching the children the Quran and serving as a general secretary to the jma'a. In addition to his salary, the ḍalb received donations from the parents of all the children sent to him for religious instruction; each father had to send ½ moud[13] of grain yearly and some rendered butter in the spring. Furthermore, a number of animals were assigned by the jma'a to the timizgida, and a shepherd was hired to look after them. The milk was consumed by the fqih and any other needy person in the douar. Some of these animals were sold periodically and the money was used to meet collective expenses: paying the salary of the fqih, donations to a passing sharif, or a gift to a nearby shrine. Travellers in the area, unmarried shepherds, and refugees in the douar could be housed in the timizgida, the different families of the douar taking turns providing them with meals.

Informants said that two or three small douars would often cooperate and set up one timizgida to serve them all. To have a mosque in one's community was a sign of prestige and religiosity; this was especially important to the Ndhiris who were always accused by the Fassis as being *kuffar* (irreligious). However, it is obvious that these tent-mosques served an important economic function in the community as well as a religious one. In fact, they seem to have functioned in very much the same manner as do mosques in the Islamic urban society. It is interesting to note that the land on which these mosques were pitched was referred to as the *hrm*, very much in the same way as Mekka and its immediate environs was classified as *al-ḥaram* (the forbidden), a special land category in Islam.

Besides the tawellat and the timizgida, there existed another institution of cooperative activity among the Ait Ndhir, the *tiwizi*. The tiwizi was voluntary cooperation among members of the douar or a larger group to help in clearing fields, putting up new tents, or digging a canal. The man who asked for the tiwizi had to provide the volunteers with tea and a meal. French officers took the tiwizi to mean a collective corvée which tribal notables could impose on their tribesmen. Guided by this interpretation, the qaids, installed by the French, ordered the Ait Ndhir to clear roads, clean up colons' fields, and work on the land of the qaids. The Ndhiris recall this with resentment and claim that it was a subversion of the indigenous institution, adding that in "the old days," only tribal chiefs could call for an obligatory tiwizi, and that this right could only be exercised in time of war.

[13] One moud = 36 liters, which is approximately one bushel. A bushel of wheat = 60 pounds; a bushel of barley = 48 pounds.

IV

SOCIOPOLITICAL ORGANIZATION

THE following chapter is devoted to an analysis of the social structure of the Ait Ndhir. The discussion is arranged in two major sections: the first focuses on the establishment of a model illustrating the nature of the corporate units making up the sociopolitical framework of the tribe, while the second section examines the dynamics of intra-tribal relationships.

ALTERNATIVE FRAMEWORKS: SEGMENTATION VERSUS ALLIANCE

To explain the mechanism for maintaining order among acephalously organized tribes, ethnologists have advanced two general theories: segmentary structure and alliance system. There is no need here to expound in detail the theory of segmentation, as it has been described and illustrated by many ethnologists.[1] It is sufficient to point out some of its major features: the encapsulation of smaller segments in larger and more inclusive ones, the interplay of balance and opposition between the different segments, the corporate nature of segments, and the jural unity of the minimal segment, the lineage.

The theory of the alliance system as the order maintaining mechanism in tribal structures is generally less well known. The most elaborate statement of this theory for North African tribes in general and for Moroccan tribes in particular is found in the work of Robert Montagne (1930). Although Montagne's theory has been criticized by several ethnologists including, most recently, Ernest Gellner, his analysis of the inherent instability and alterations of

---

[1]The classic work on the theory of segmentation remains E. Evans-Pritchard's *The Nuer* (1940). See also E. Evans-Pritchard, *The Sanusi of Cyranaica* (1949); M. G. Smith, "Segmentary Lineage Systems", (1956:39-81); M. D. Sahlins, "The Segmentary Lineage: An Organization of Predatory Expansion" in R. Cohen and J. Middleton (eds.), *Comparative Political Systems* (1967:89-119).

the Berber tribal structure remains significant enough to be considered in any discussion of tribalism in Morocco.[2]

Montagne's political theory is based on the assumption that normally the Berber populations were organized in a mosaic of small, independent, and autonomous "republics" (what Montagne calls canton, his translation of the Berber word, *taqbilt*). These republics were made up of hierarchies of petty notables or patriarchs who sat on an assembly that directed the daily affairs of each group. At the top of the social hierarchy were the chiefs, *imzran*, to whom was entrusted the management of the affairs of the whole tribe, or canton. Daily life within the canton was characterized by endemic feuding. This conflict, which varied in magnitude and significance, was regulated through the interplay of the alliance system, *leff* (from the Arabic *laffa*, to wrap around). The leff was perceived by Montagne to be a basic structural feature of the tribal organization,[3] each unit or segment within the canton was incorporated into one or the other of the two major alliances that prevailed over all the Western High Atlas mountains. The primary function of this dual alliance system was to act as a brake on the possible amplification of conflict both within and beyond the individual cantons. The leff pattern, according to Montagne, was a permanently constituted, territorially discontinuous league that made of the whole region a huge checkerboard of alliances. As long as the Berber chiefs remained party to these alliances, their power and influence remained limited and circumscribed; a booty gained in war had to be shared with all the partners in the leff, thus automatically limiting the resources of any one successful war chief. Therefore, adds Montagne, in order for a chief to gain freedom to maneuver and the liberty to dispense with resources as he pleased, he must dominate the two leffs; in other words, he must render the alliance system inoperative. This could be accomplished by manipulating a local conflict and assassinating rival chiefs. Having achieved that goal, the chief could impose his power both on his own tribe and on the neighboring ones as well. He would emerge as a paramount chief or *amghar*, an absolute ruler of a miniature domain whose boundaries usually coincide with the limits of the original leff system. In order for the amghar to further consolidate his power, he would then turn to the Sultan and seek to be confirmed as his agent, qaid. The Sultan would usually give his consent reluctantly and in essence, a small makhzan would

---

[2] Montagne's theory anticipates the gumsa-gumlao theory elaborated by Edmund R. Leach for the tribes of Highland Burma in *Political Systems of Highland Burma*, (London, 1964).

[3] Montagne, along with most French ethnologists of Morocco, did not employ the concept of segmentation in his approach to tribal structure; see Jeanne Favret (1968:105-111).

then have been duplicated in the remote mountains. "Le but souvent inconscient, des efforts des chefs et du sultan est achever (ainsi) la fondation, sur les ruines des cantons berbères, d'un Empire absolu, sans frontières intérieures, soumis a une loi unique et qui condamne les sujets a subir une ruineuse et impitoyable tyrannie" (Montagne, 1930:391). This tyranny comes to an end when, in the aftermath of one of the periodic national dynastic crises, the Berbers seek an end to their subjugation, overthrow their qaid, and return to their traditional anarchy.

Designed originally to explain the rise to power of the "Grand Caids" of the Western Atlas, Montagne expanded his theory, especially that of the leff, to explain the history and social structure of all the Berber tribes. He was taken to task by Jacques Berque, who found no such permanent alliance pattern among the Seksawa. David Hart (1973) and Ernest Gellner (1969) have recently questioned the pervasiveness and stability of these alliances. Gellner grants the possibility that permanent checkerboard alliances are present in some regions, but adds that "if and when it [the alliance system] exists, it is not the crux of the matter; it is only relevant to one level of segmentation, and it is only one further, albeit intriguing kink and variant in the segmentary structure, which is itself the crucial order-maintaining mechanism" (1969:67).

The crux of the matter, according to Gellner, is the fact that the Berber tribes are organized in a "pure segmentary system" which actually operates. Gellner did his research among a saintly tribe in the middle High Atlas, the zawiya Ahansal, and his book is primarily concerned with illustrating the indispensable religious and political role that is played by a set of holy lineages who are situated among the segmented Berbers of the region. In fact, Gellner concludes that it is through the display of their religious charisma, *baraka*, and the enactment of their structurally intermediate role that these "inegalitarian, stratified, pacific, 'artificial' outsiders played functions which enabled the egalitarian, feud-addicted tribesmen to work their remarkably pure segmentary system" (1969:66). Having rejected the role of alliances as the crucial order-maintaining mechanism, Gellner demonstrates that it is the relationship between saintliness and segmented structure which maintains order in a society where endemic feuding threatens to become virtual anarchy.

Gellner deals almost exclusively with the highest level of segmentation and rarely concerns himself with the specific social principles that order and direct social interaction between the individual tribesmen. He does not propose to examine the alliances and contractual bonds that arise at lower levels of segmentation and that often take precedence over the segmentary order. Gellner mentions this possibility, but dismisses its significance: "Alliances do take place and links are established in addition to the segmentary alignment, but these additions form no system" (1969:66). Since they form no system, alliances and contractual bonds are relegated to the category of "intriguing kinks."

Gellner's analysis still leaves unresolved the question of whether one can adequately characterize all Berber tribes by an examination of the saintly tribes and a logical analysis of the "pure segmentary system" without taking into account all the kinks and variants that modify and perhaps render this pure system operable. As the following discussion will illustrate, the Ait Ndhir seem to have operated simultaneously in terms of the two models, segmentary and alliance (considered as pure types). They did so without suffering the strain and stress of the ethnologist who tends to view these systems as contradictory and incompatible. Both verbally and behaviorally, the Ait Ndhir made no effort to be consistent and did not therefore place either individuals or groups in straitjackets or segmentary and/or alliance behavior restrictions. This normative flexibility and structural openness allowed them to survive as a Tamazight tribe until the coming of the French.

WHAT WAS AN AIT NDHIR TRIBE?

An Organization for Anarchy

The Ait Ndhir divide all Moroccan tribes into three categories:

(1) *guish*—those tribes who were allied to the government;
(2) *naiba*—those tribes who were too weak to resist the government;
(3) *taryazt*—those tribes who were free and independent.[4]

They themselves were always a taryazt tribe: "We came from the south and fought our way through the mountains with the guns (*bilbarood*), and we took this land with the gun. We kept it with our guns and later we were driven off it only with the cannon (*nfaḍ*)."[5] However, this pride in their past independence does not

---

[4]*Naiba* was a replacement tax that certain tribes paid in return for the use of makhzan land. They also furnished contingents to the Sultan on an irregular basis. *Taryazt* is from the Berber *aryaz* = man, warrior, manly.

[5]This is a reference to the French army who used heavy cannons against the tribe.

yield any concrete knowledge of their tribal structure or history. Oral tradition is minimal in the society and what there is does not explain origins nor does it validate structural relationships. "People call us Ait Ndhir; and it is our name. It is the same way that we call other groups near us Ait Youssi or Zayan. Or the same way you say Fransis (French)." Others, more sophisticated, would say, "There must have been a man called Ndhir who was our ancestor and the founder of this tribe, but we really do not know anything about him except that he must have lived in the south because that is where we came from." One informant, a literate man (Ait Sliman), supplied the following story which was told him by a grandfather:

> At the time of the Prophet, there lived three brothers, one of whom was called Ndhir. One brother died and then Ndhir killed the other brother. The jma'a [tribal assembly] met and decided that Ndhir should be put to death for having committed the crime of fratricide. But he ran away and came to Tunis. However, he did not stay in Tunis for a long time, but left and made his way to the Maghreb and came to the south near the town of Rish, where he married a tamazight [Berber] woman and became the founder of the Ait Ndhir.

The Ndhiris claim that the Arabic version of their name, Beni Mtir, was given them by a sharif from Fez who reputedly exclaimed, "hadi mashi Ait Ndhir, hadi albla kaytir" (this is no tribe of Ait Ndhir, this is the scourge that flies) (see Appendix I). This is in reference to their notorious banditry and mobility on horseback as they retreated into the mountains. "And from that day on, the name stuck to us and came to replace our Berber name."

The Ait Ndhir are patrilineal and segmentary. They refer to themselves as a *taqbilt*, the term being the tamazight form of the Arabic word, *qabila*: tribe and/or confederation. They do not claim descent from one ancestor and their usual reply to the question, "Why are you a taqbilt?" is "Because we share an area in common, have one dialect [i.e. speak differently from the way the Zayan and Gerwan do] and have our own *qa'ida* [custom]." The term "taqbilt" among the Ait Ndhir is reserved for the supreme unit with which the individual identifies and is never utilized in a sliding segmentary fashion, i.e., relative to context as is reported for such other Middle Atlas tribes as the Ait Ayash.[6] As far as I could ascertain, the Ait Ndhir usage holds true for all of the dir tribes and may reflect the political ascendency of that level (confederation)

---

[6]Information supplied by Mr. John Chiapuris.

in their chronic wars with the makhzan.[7] The Ait Ndhir are familiar with the term *khams-khmas* (five fifths) which has been translated to mean "a confederation."[8] However, they reserve the term for such large, powerful, and predatory political confederacies as the Ait Atta of the Sahara, the Zayan, and the Beni Mguild. They say that the Zayan were a khams-khmas because you could divide the taqbilt into five parts and each one could stand on its own as if it were taqbilt. To the Ait Ndhir, the term khams-khmas conveys the idea of a super-confederation, which they say they never were. I would rather have translated the term "taqbilt" among the Ndhir to mean a confederation, and elevated the next level of segmentation, the primary *ighs*, to that of a tribe, especially when one considers that these were independent of one another, had their own territory (there was no territory considered to be jointly owned by the Ait Ndhir), and each had its own customary law (*izref* or *'urf*). But this would have been going against accepted usage and would have led to further and perhaps unnecessary confusion. It has been suggested that the Ait Ndhir represented the remnants of the shattered Ait Idrassen confederation and was therefore a group that had lost its original manifest segmentary organization and strong sense of solidarity (Burke, 1968). This may be the case, but the fact does remain that they were a viable society coping extremely well with their political and physical environments. This adaptation was in terms of a specific sociopolitical system that may prove to be a variation of a generalized Middle Atlas type.

The term "taqbilt" therefore connotes the largest political framework that encompasses a number of contiguous groups, all exploiting common ecological zones, in this case, the complementary zones of transhumance—the plateau and the plain. The major role of the taqbilt was to safeguard the strategic and economic area necessary for the proper functioning of these groups as well as representing their common interest vis-à-vis other groups of the same order.

The Primary Segments of the Tribe

There are 10 primary divisions within the taqbilt. These are named, territorially localized segments of equal structural order

---

[7] It is interesting to note that the Berbers seem to have no indigenous terms for the largest cooperating political groups, but utilize Arabic ones. The Kabyles use *thakelbilt*, while Riffis use *tishourkt*, from the Arabic *sharaka*, to share.

[8] For a discussion of the five fifths, see D. M. Hart, "Segmentary Systems and the Role of 'five fifths' in Tribal Morocco", *Revue de l'Occident musulman et de la Mediterranean.* no. 3, 1967, p. 65-95.

called *ikhsan* (sing. *ighs*). The French refer to this level of segmentation as "fraction," and it has been translated as "clan" (Gellner, 1969:93; Abes, 1918: 40). The word "ighs" means "bone" in Tamazight and the Ait Ndhir, who tend to be bilingual in Arabic (especially the men) use the term *fekhda* (thigh) and *ferqa* (division) when speaking of this level. Ighs is the Ndhiri segmentary designate par excellence; it is used to refer to all subsequent tribal subdivisions regardless of size and rank, although at lower levels they generally substitute the diminutive form *tighst* (pl. *tikhsatin*). The 10 ikhsan of the Ait Ndhir are:

(1) Ait Iqqedaren
(2) Ait Bourzouine
(3) Ait Sliman
(4) Ait Lahcen ou Sháib
(5) Ait Boubidman
(6) Ait Ourtindi
(7) Ait Hammad
(8) Ait Ouallal Bittit
(9) Ait Harzallah
(10) Ait Na'aman

The above are the original and "real" sections to which the French later added two more: Ait Ayash and Ait Lahcen Bou Youssef. The Ait Ndhir point out that the Ait Ayash are a clan of the Ait Ayash of the Anseghmir. In 1803, Mawlay Sliman defeated the Idrassen and in the aftermath detached a section of the Ait Ayash and brought them to the Sais plain. The Ait Lahcen Bou Youssef is a recent composite group made up of some Ait Na'aman families and some Mjjat who were relocated by the French on land owned originally by the Na'aman.

Figure 8 illustrates a typical segmentary organization among the Ait Ndhir. The usual depth varies between three and four levels; younger informants are completely ignorant of levels III and IV, whereas older ones tend to disagree on which tigemmi are to be included in what tighst. Most of the ikhsan on levels III and IV tend to bear names that imply agnatic descent, but in the absence of genealogies, they serve only for identification purposes. Apart from the primary sections (level I), all others above the level of tigemmi can be considered as contingent groups, since as far as could be ascertained, they had no jural, political, or ritual functions. They are there logically by virtue of the segmentary principle, but remained structurally and functionally latent. They may be considered as

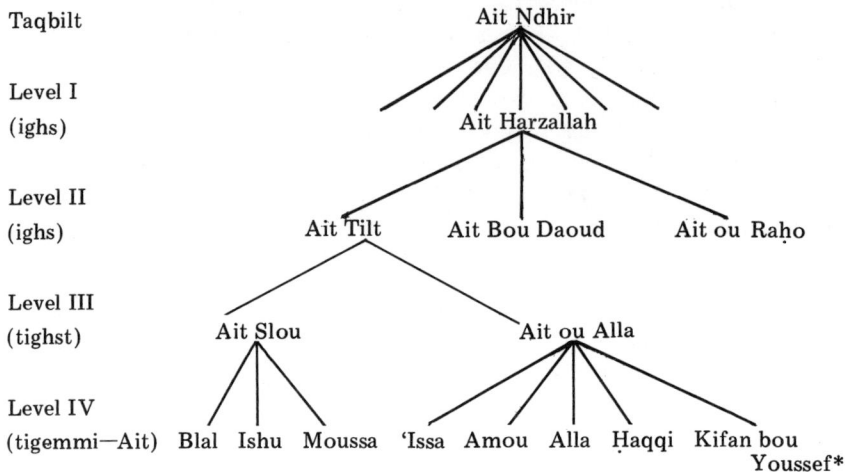

*Kifan bou Youssef is composed today exclusively of shurfa Boukili families.

Fig. 8. The segmentary organization of the Ait Harzallah (only the subdivisions indicated for levels I and IV are exhaustive).

nominal descent groups, since above the level of the douar, putative common descent is the generalized deduction from the possession of the common name. The Ait Ndhir appear to be incapable of idiomatically perceiving their social structure in any terms other than those of agnatic descent.

There are no written genealogies among the tribe and I was unable to collect more than very shallow and incomplete ones. Elders readily admit that they never kept genealogies and furthermore consider the whole subject irrelevant. They say that each ighs "must" be based on a core of agnates and their descendants, but when genealogies are elicited, the usual answer is "Why should we keep genealogies?" And, in fact, they do not need to. Unilineal descent does not validate itself ceremonially or economically. Being self-consciously Berber on the edge of Arab territory, they were cut off from the Arab-sharifian monopoly of baraka and its exploitation for economic profit; Fez and Meknes exported more than their share of shurfa and fqihs, not to mention those who came from the south. Furthermore, the principles of equality of all adults in the ighs, the lack of primogeniture, the collective ownership of land, and the disinheritance of females all contribute to the lack of emphasis on unilineal descent, except as a convenient principle for primary recruitment to the group. Generally speaking, agnatic descent among the Ait Ndhir is more a variable than a parameter of their social structure. Its major function is to define the status and legitimacy of individuals and groups in terms of their access to common resources and the rights and duties of each group, both in relation to one another and to the resources. The primary role of agnatic descent is not group formation, recruitment, or maintenance. To the question, "How do you determine who is and who is not an Ait Ndhir?," the elders reply, "If he fights with us he is our brother."

As will be discussed shortly, there were several contractual arrangements through which a stranger (*barrani*, lit.: outsider) could be fully incorporated into the tribe. It is interesting that today the question of who is a real Ait Ndhir has become an important and complex issue. This is especially so among clans that have retained large amounts of collective land and who are now demographically pressed for space. The group would like to divide this joint patrimony, and in its self-interest is seeking to eliminate all the "strangers" and bar them from access to the land. As an old man of Ait Harzallah said,

> In the old days, people came from other tribes, made the *tamghrost* [sacrifice] and we let them settle on our land. In time they took their guns and fought along our side and they became our brothers. Now everybody is selfish and people point out this and that *takhamt* [lit. tent, but the term is still used to refer to an extended family] and say "they are not genuine Harzallawis; we remember their grandfather who came from the Riff and was allowed to squat on our land. He did not even make the tamghrost. They cannot be counted on us [meaning they cannot be considered as members of the group when it comes to division of collective land]." This is *ḥshuma* (shame) and against the *qa'ida* [custom]. But then things have changed and many of us who never have farmed in our lives are obliged to take up the plough and break the rocks for a living.

The 10 clans[9] may be considered corporate to the extent that they were permanently constituted, land-owning units. Ndhiris insist that there were and always will be 10 ikhsan (clans) to their taqbilt. The land was considered the collective property of all male members of the ighs, who had only usufructuary rights to it. It was called *tamazirt-n jma't* (the land of the collectivity or group). If a man left his clan territory for a period of time he held residual rights to it which could be activated upon his return; but if he left his family behind, they were considered to be "using his share."

---

[9] These 10 primary segments of the Ait Ndhir, ikhsan, are simultaneously referred to as clans, tribal segments, fractions, or factions.

Women had no independent legal status in the society; their access to resources was defined by their roles as mothers, wives, and daughters. Under certain circumstances, however, they could constitute a sort of "carrier" of tribal rights, and could serve as links to perpetuate the patrilineal family in the absence of males.[10] There were two ways in which this was done, the *amḥars* (lit.: one who is watched or guarded) and *amazzal* (from the Berber verb amz, to catch, to take) relationships. A widowed woman with young sons might find a man whom she would marry informally (i.e., without the public sacrifice) and who would become the head of her family. She then operated an independent household, one not incorporated into her former husband's household, and any children born to her out of the new marriage were considered ("counted on") her deceased husband's. In other words, the new sons retained rights to the collective property of the clan of the former husband, regardless of the actual affiliation of the progenitor, who was known as amazzal. The second arrangement was more formalized. A man, who might be an outsider to the taqbilt, would come to the jma'a (assembly) of a douar and make a sacrifice (tamghrost). He would ask to become an amḥars of someone in the group. One of those present would then agree to be his sponsor and a contract period between the two would then be decided upon publicly. Such a period would usually range between two and six years. During this time, the amḥars would live near his patron, who would usually give him a daughter or niece in marriage. Any children born would be considered the mother's, that is, belonging to the patron's lineage. The amḥars would not be allowed to marry a second wife until his contract period was over, and, should he die, his accumulated goods would go to his patron. If, at the end of the contract period, the man decided to move away, he would have to leave his wife and children behind. But should he decide to stay permanently, he would be "adopted" into the group. The amḥars would take a sheep and sacrifice it in front of the jma'a of the douar and declare his desire to join the taqbilt "as a free man." They would then give him a piece of land on which he could set up an independent household with his wife and children. But before settling, he would pay a bride price to his former patron and thus achieve full status. He could then sit in the jma'a, carry arms, and participate in wars; he also became liable for the payment of the *diyya* (blood money) like any other member of the douar.

[10]This need not be literally true. Informants say that if the takhamat has only a few males, it is weak *(d'eef)* and must therefore be augmented.

Both the amazzal and the amḥars were considered as *amzaid*, i.e., people who were added to the original group. A slight social stigma was attached to the status since it implied that the amzaid lacked full *aryazen* (manly, gun carrying tribesman) status in his own tribe. However, subsequent personal success and prestige could obliterate the initial *miskin* (abject, servile) stigma. Children of amzaids who were later incorporated into the douars suffered no handicap whatsoever.

Apart from the Quranic injunctions, the Ait Ndhir had no preferential or proscribed marriage rules. They knew of the Arab tribes' preference for the father's brother's daughter, but stated that it was not their way (*abrid*) or custom (qa'ida). The best marriages were those within the clan since "we share the same customs and there is less likelihood for the woman to run away." Clans who bordered other tribes often exchanged women, e.g. the Iqeddaren exchanged women with the Irklaouen clan of the Beni Mguild. But this was simply a function of proximity and personal preference rather than any systematic alliance-making activity. In general, marriage was not a pivotal institution in the political system, and women were not considered a terribly important commodity. Often they were "inherited" along with other movable property. Ndhiri women claim that their status is better today, since under the shari'a they can at least appoint a *wakil* (representative) who will represent their interests in court or in disputes.

The lack of preferred marriage patterns among the tribe resulted in the absence of common genealogical unity at any level above that of the extended family or the minimal lineage. This, and the practice of open recruitment into the agnatic descent group, rendered them structurally flexible. Logically, one could elevate the descent-organized segmentary constructs among the Ait Ndhir into a model of the social system, but such a model would not refer to anything real or relevant to the Ndhiris themselves, or to the functioning of their society. This is not to deny the idiomatic prevalence of kinship terminology and concepts. For example, no matter what the original form of incorporation into the group, in time it will be reinterpreted in agnatic terms.

The Camping Unit: Tigemmi

The *tigemmi* was the smallest and the most viable segment among the Ait Ndhir. French writers rightly refer to it as the cell at the base of the social organization. The term tigemmi, which today is completely replaced by douar, referred to a group of tents that camped together. Their number varied between 14 and 25. Ndhiris say that the ideal tigemmi should have had no less than 20 adult men, which was usually enough to repel a sudden raid. A tigemmi of fewer than 13 men was considered to be "weak" and should have either increased its number or joined up with another one. An extended family which formed one economic household was considered one takhamat, "tent," regardless of its actual size; thus the Ndhiris use the term for tent coupled to an individual's name to mean "the house of so and so." For example, *Ait ukham Haddou ou Ali* refers to an extended family headed by Haddou ou Ali. The family owned all the animals in common and exploited one share of the irrigated land. Upon the death of Haddou, it could break up and form as many takhamats as Haddou had sons; or the sons might decide not to divide and to stay together as one household. A group of closely related takhamats formed a rif. The number of rifs varied with the size of the tigemmi and they say that when a rif grew too large, it simply broke away to form a new tigemmi. This new tigemmi became a replica of the original one; no genealogical depth was added.

The actual composition of the tigemmi varied seasonally. In winter and when the group was in the lowland, it conformed closely to the ideal model. A tigemmi would consist of an agnatically related group, of three to four generations in depth, that had definite jural character since it was liable for the payment of a joint diyya (blood money) and was directed by an assembly. In summer, though, greater flexibility was displayed; an original tigemmi might split up and each rif could band with a different group and spend the summer months travelling in the higher pastures. These temporary camp units were based on personal preferences, affinal ties, and economic cooperation. The Ait Ndhir had institutionalized means for forging these non-descent based units and some of these will be discussed further on.

Each tigemmi was alloted an area on the plain. This area was then divided up among the different households.[11] Plots were divided equally regardless of the actual size of the household or the number of draft animals that it possessed. In theory, plots were rotated annually, but in practice this was not done until some drastic change in the douar's composition necessitated a redivision. It should be pointed out that the Ndhiris possessed more arable land

---

[11] The normal procedure was for the jma'a of the douar to go into the fields, survey an area, and then divide it *bilhabl*, i.e. using a rope for measurement.

than they could utilize, and that agriculture was in any case a subsidiary activity in their total economy. The French counted 18,099 Ait Ndhir in the year 1915. These were spread out over an area totalling approximately 1,500 square kilometers, giving them a rough density of 12 people per square kilometer. Their occupation of the area on the plain was normally precarious and conditional since they could be and often were driven off it by the sultans. However, their hold on their territory on the plateau was more tenacious and significant to them in terms of pasture for their animals and the strategic function of the area in case of retreat. This grazing area (*agdal*) was never divided up; it was exploited jointly by all of the tigemmi.[12]

The tigemmi constituted the most visible and critical level of organization among the Ait Ndhir; it was the unit in which the jural, kinship, and territorial principles of the society intersected. Tigemmis had a remarkable degree of autonomy; they resembled tribes in miniature. Only when the group was at war did the tigemmis recede in importance, giving way to the level that was the most operative politically, the ighs.

The Assembly of Elders: Jma'a

The day-to-day affairs of the tigemmi were directed by an informal assembly of men, the jma'a. All adult males in the douar were theoretically eligible to sit on the assembly; the insane, sick, women, and children were excluded. So were the *barranis*, the outsiders. In practice, however, a usual *jma'a n tigemmi* consisted of five to seven older men who had authority and commanded respect in their community. The Ndhiris call them *akhatar* (pl. *ikhataren*). The ikhataren met irregularly to deal with problems as they arose. Since most activities were routine, the major function of the jma'a was the regulation and containment of conflict. French ethnographers tend to elevate the jma'a into a specialized political institution with defined roles and functions. In fact, the jma'a did not constitute a specialized political body, but was simply the extension of the patriarchal kinship system. It was not so much a well-defined institution as a mode of expression of the solidarity of the small agnatically based group; it had no regular meeting days and no hierarchy. It functioned through the tacit agreement of the whole group. An *akhatar n jma't* (or as they call him, an *ajemma'i*, one

---

[12] I have been using the terms douar and tigemmi interchangeably. Today the term douar is used indiscriminantly to refer to all types of rural settlements in Morocco. See the special issues of the *Revue de Geographie*, no. 8, 1965.

who is a member of the jma'a) was neither elected nor appointed to his position. He was there because the sum total of all the roles he played in his community made him a natural and informal leader and spokesman for the group. The jma'a functioned as both a judicial and administrative body; it allocated collective land, oversaw division of water for irrigation, collected money for a passing sharif, and officiated at marriages and inheritance ceremonies. Above all, it served as guardian of the qa'ida or the customary way of the life of the community.[13]

Tribal Leaders: Amghar

The jma'a of the ighs was composed of members coopted from the jma'as of each douar. This jma'a usually numbered 18 to 20 persons. Members met irregularly to handle matters that affected the whole clan; hence their duties were mainly political in nature. They decided on alliances, concluded peace pacts (*hana*), and coordinated the summer grazing movements of the douars. When necessary, they negotiated with tribes that pastured on territory of the Ait Ndhir during severe winters, groups such as the Beni Mguild and the Seghrouchen. They also elected the amghar (chief) for the whole clan. "The ikhataren met in a tent; they sacrificed and ate sheep. They then talked and went outside, so everybody could see them and chose one among themselves to be the amghar.[14] Then each akhatar took some grass and put it on him saying, 'We have chosen you to be our amghar and we shall obey you.' The amghar then turned and said, 'Give me the *amasais* [the respondents] who will be responsible for you' and we sent him those that he wanted. The amghar was chosen from war to war." Actually, each ighs usually nominated one person for the position of amghar, and if the jma'a did not agree on a choice, then they selected by lot (*ghir illan*).[15]

The amasi was a person chosen by the douar to "speak for them" and to be responsible for their behavior to the amghar. At the same time, he must be acceptable to the amghar. Ndhiris usually use the Arabic term *ḍhamen* (guarantor) to refer to the amasai.

---

[13] Ndhiris use the term qa'ida (Arabic custom) and abrid (Berber road, way) to refer to the traditional way of life of the tribe. The terms izref and 'urf are used to refer to the customary laws that safeguard and embody these traditions.

[14] Informants always mentioned "going outside, so all can see" as an integral part of all ceremonies and group meetings. This public witness as validation was no doubt necessary in an illiterate society.

[15] There seems to have been no systematic method for electing the amghar among the Ait Ndhir, certainly nothing like the rotation and complementarity mentioned by Gellner for the Central High Atlas (1969:81). In cases where the members of the jma'a disagreed on a candidate, they took a number of straws of equal length and included a short one among them. Then each ajemma'i pulled a straw and the man who got the short one got to name the amghar.

SOCIOPOLITICAL ORGANIZATION 65

"The amasai made sure that he was chosen by everybody in the tigemmi. He then told them 'now you have to obey me' and they said, 'yes, we have chosen you and we shall obey you.'" The amasai stood responsible for his douar to the amghar; when the amghar gave an order, especially in wartime, he had to be obeyed. If a man disobeyed, then the amghar ordered the man's amasai to burn his tent or to cut his wife's hair in public (see Appendix II). Amasais left their *silham* (outer garment) with the amghar; if they failed in their duties or made trouble, the women dyed them *henna* (yellow) and exhibited them outside the tent. This was *'ar* (grave shame).

Each clan usually had one amghar; occasionally two powerful leaders might contest the title; the clan would then split into factions. Ait Ndhir tended to refer to their amghars as *amghar al barood* (the war chief) rather than *amghar n touya* (chief of the grass), which is the usual form among the Middle Atlas tribes in general.[16] Also, whereas in other areas, the amghar served for a one year term, the Ait Ndhir insisted that there was no time limit set on their own amghars; they could serve as long as they were judged to be successful in their role. Amghars were not paid directly.

> L'amghar n'est pas rétribué. Pour le dédommager de ses peines, de sa responsabilité, et des frais d'hospitalité qu'exigent ses fonctions, il jouit de certains avantages. Les groupements désignent en effet des hommes qui exécutent ce qu'on appelle "les corvées d'amghar"; on lui laboure ses champes, on moisonne et on dépique sa récolte ... on porte son courrier a destination, on garde ses tentes. De plus, il touche les amendes (en berbère: izmaz) infligées à ceux qui contreviennent à la coutume, désobéissent à l'amghar ou à ses subordonnés ... le taux des amendes est assez élevé en temps de guerre. L'amghar n'hésite pas à confisquer les biens du délinquent, a brûler sa tente, à raser les cheveux de sa femme en public (Abes, 1918:45-46).

In theory, there was a jma'a for the whole taqbilt whose members were coopted from the jma'as of each clan, and this jma'a would in turn choose a paramount amghar who was usually called amghar n touya. But despite the fact that, in the monograph written by Abes on the Ait Ndhir, such a jma'a and an amghar are mentioned (1918:45), I was not able to pinpoint any one historical point in time in which this logical extension of the sociopolitical model did in fact operate. The Ait Ndhir do not seem to have ever fought as one corporate unit. The usual pattern was for a clan or two to fight (against Gerwan or Dkhissa) while the remaining clans "stood behind them, in their backs," giving them tacit support

---

[16]Ndhiris know of the term *amghar n touya* and some used it, but the rule was to use *amghar al barood*, or simply *amghar*.

and aid. In such cases, one of the amghars involved would take over as the supreme commander (or one would be chosen on the spur of the moment) and he would be assisted by the most influential and prestigious ikhataren. Needless to say, one can hardly exaggerate the importance of the personal charisma and character of the leader in this highly ill-defined role and in the context of a nebulous shifting field of power. The closest that the Ait Ndhir came to fighting as one unit, at least within historical memory, was in the years 1908-1909, and even then the leadership was in the hands of two amghars. As the tribesmen themselves say, "the word (*klam*) of the whole taqbilt was entrusted to two people: 'Aqqa Boubidmani and Mokhtar Al-Hammadi." These two leaders became the spokesmen for the tribe. There is no doubt that despite the disproportionate amount of power given an amghar, he was still considered to be the embodiment of the collective will of the tribe and the symbol of its latent solidarity.

Perhaps the following story will elucidate both the attitude of the tribe to the amghar and the relative status of the position.

> The qaid Haddou bou Grin[17] and all those of the tribe who were allied with him were with Sidi Rahu in the mountains fighting the French. They then started to raid us, their cousins.[18] We got tired of this and all of us got together, all the different ikhsan went to Bou Semsel and chose Hajj Alilou Al-Boubidmani to be our amghar. This then meant that all the other qaids including Haddou bou Grin became as if they were the amasais of the newly chosen amghar. We then went out against Sidi Rahu and the Ndhiris with him and chased them until we reached Tichoukt (in Seghrouchen territory). We did not rely on the French to fight for us.

Rank and Status within the Tribe

Apart from the shurfa, there were no distinctions of rank within the society itself. The Ait Ndhir maintained a special relationship with zawiya Boukili which is located north of Ksar al Souk in the territory of Ait Izdig. Boukili shurfa travelled (and still do) every summer to the territory of the Ait Ndhir to collect their share of the harvest, *'ushr*. Some lingered to mediate conflict and to lend their moral presence to alliances. They also prescribed love potions for the tribesmen and dispensed curing services. No one

---

[17] An example of the inconsistency of the Ait Ndhir, who often use the terms qaid, amghar, and sheikh to refer to the same man. When questioned about this, they replied, "Haddou bou Grin was really only an amghar since we were at *siba* then."

[18] The majority of the Ait Ndhir had submitted to the French at this time since it was harvest time on the plain and they did not dare leave their crops to be burned by the French army.

knows exactly when this symbiotic relationship started between the zawiya and the tribe, but informants claim that it dates back to the time when the tribe was still in the south.[19] In fact, one whole douar among the Ait Harzallah (kifan bou Youssef) is composed entirely of shurfa Boukilis who have been settled among the Harzallah for at least 100 years. These are inactive shurfa with no manifest baraka. In the old days they refrained from carrying arms, but otherwise were hardly distinguishable from the rest. A certain amount of deference is granted them today by older Ndhiris and they themselves make feeble attempts at confirming their separate rank. Thus they tend to be endogamous, seclude their women, and forbid them from mingling with crowds at public celebrations.

Positions of status were few and, with the exception of the amghars, highly generalized. Personal character was of real and paramount importance since it was relevant to the requirements of leadership: self-confidence, dignity, exercise of judgment, and responsibility. All leaders were subsumed under the category of ikhataren, out of which were chosen the amghars, amasais, and ajemma'is. All ikhataren, almost by definition, commanded great personal prestige and enjoyed public trust, which served as their weapons in the absence of ritual sanctions and coercive power. Whenever the jma'a of any level met, members had to be present unless they had valid reasons for absence. Complete attendance was necessary to lend the weight of general consensus to resolutions; those individuals who failed to appear had to kill a sheep and host the jma'a for a day.

Even though the amghar did monopolize the right to exercise certain extremes of force, such as burning a tent or cutting the hair of women, his position was nevertheless one of relative authority and not of arbitrary power. The jma'a continually evaluated his performance and, when necessary, could remove him. "Good" amghars have been known to last 10 years; "bad" ones could be impeached immediately. Distortions in this flexibility were often the result of the makhzan's interference.

> We had this amghar whom the jma'a had elected. One day he sent for an amasai and told him, "go to your people and get me 20 mounted men with guns. I need them." We were not at war, and the amasai went and told the other people. The ikhataren then got up and came to the qasba

---

[19] A story gathered by John Chiapuris among the Ait Haddidou explains the origin of the relationship in this way: "The Ait Ndhir [Beni Mtir] were a wicked and mischievous tribe. One day all the saints gathered to read the *fatiha* and to plan how to eliminate the Ait Ndhir. Only Sidi Boukil spoke up for them and asked the saints to spare them; he promised that he will try to control them. Because of this, the Ait Ndhir visit the zawiya of Sidi Boukil, which is located higher than the River Ziz near Rish. They offer the saint sheep, mules, butter, and grain."

of El Hajeb to see why the amghar was giving such orders. They found him with 200 'askar (soldiers) that the Sultan had sent him. Now they knew that he was a real qaid and nobody could disobey, not with 200 soldiers at his command.[20]

THE DYNAMICS OF INTRA-TRIBAL RELATIONSHIPS

"A good war justified any cause."

The normal relationship between the ikhsan was one of mutual suspicion and hostility since they were rivals for land and for the right to protect travellers and caravans that passed through tribal territory. Warfare expressed the political legitimacy of the ighs and it therefore necessarily mobilized all individuals within the territory of the clan. It also formed the only occasion on which the cohesion of the whole group became visible.[21] As mentioned earlier, the harshest measures were dealt out to those who disobeyed the amghar or who refused to fight. Since the tribe had no high centralized authority to mediate and to end the continual raids and warring between its primary segments (they themselves say that a supreme amghar tended always to favor his own group), they resorted to outsiders: shurfa, famous arbitrators from nearby tribes, and often the Sultan himself.

> We had been fighting among ourselves for a long time and we were tired; but we could not agree. So a delegation of notables went to Fez to seek the audiences of the Sultan Mawlay Hassan. He met them and said to them, "Why is it that you, the Ait Ndhir, are always fighting among yourselves? The news had reached me that you make the roads unsafe for caravans, your fields rest fallow, and your crops unharvested while you fight; why do you do this?" Then one of the notables present, the qaid Hammou Al-Hajj said, "Mawlana, it may be we fight because the clans (afkhad) are all intermingled on the land." And the Sultan said, "Why don't you go back and separate the different afkhads and put each one on its own territory with its own boundaries?" And the notables thought it was a good idea and when they came back here, they did just that. They got together all the jma'as and worked out the boundaries; and from that day all the Iqeddaren are on this land and all the

---

[20] This story was told to me by an Iqeddaren who claims that the amghar in question was his great uncle. The Sultan mentioned was Mawlay Hassan. The informant said that the amghar had promised the Sultan to make his ighs (the Iqeddaren) a guish tribe in the service of the makhzan. In return for this and to insure that the amghar would implement the plan, the Sultan sent him the soldiers and also some guns and uniforms. However, adds the informant, his uncle soon changed his mind and the bargain was never fulfilled.

[21] The clan territory was considered an extension of the solidarity of the human group itself, and a measure of its strength—in other words, an affirmation of their right to be. Ndhiris say, "Our land was our strength."

Harzallah are on that. And they did not fight as much because of the advice of the Sultan, who was a wise man.[22]

The Ait Ndhir know of the word leff (which is the usual North African term for alliance), but do not use it. They say that it is an Arabic word which simply means alliance, the power that an individual or group can muster in case of a quarrel. They have their own word for alliance: *thamunt* or *thumint*. Etymologically, the word "thamunt" or its variant "thumint" may be derived either from the verb *amn*, which is Arabic meaning "safety" or "security," or from the Tamazight verb *mun*, meaning "to accompany." Either way, it makes semantic sense. The Ait Ndhir use "thamunt" in a generic fashion to mean "an alliance"; they then differentiate between several kinds of alliances, each involving its own sanctions and responsibilities. The most important of these alliances was the *taḍa*.

In reply to a question about the number of clans in the tribe, an old and intelligent informant replied, "Well, you could say there are five and you could say there are 10. It all depends on how you look at it. If you are looking from above, then we are five and I will show you how." He then proceeded to count in pairs, "Ait Hammad and Ait Harzallah, Ait Boubidman and Ait Ourtindi, Ait Sliman and Ait Bourzouine, Ait Lahcen ou Shaib and Ait Iqeddar, Ait Oullal and Ait Naʻaman. Now each of these pairs had a thamunt between them, therefore we could be considered five divisions." The thamunt implied mutual assistance and the sharing of clan territory. Each of the pairs mentioned occupied a different altitude and the alliance obviously functioned therefore to provide the necessary complementarity of areas for transhumance. Furthermore, this vague alliance pattern among the clans precipitated itself into an overall dual division of the tribe into two halves, what the Ndhiris call the *Ait Omnaṣf* (Omnaṣf = half). Thus, one Ait Omnaṣf was made up of the clans of Ouallal, Naʻaman, Harzallah, Boubidman, Hammad, and Ourtindi, as opposed to the other Ait Omnaṣf made up of the Iqeddaren, Bourzouine, Lahcen ou Shaib, and Sliman. These also corresponded very roughly to an East-West geographical division.

It is claimed that when intra-tribal wars occurred, the clans fell

---

[22]Regardless of the authenticity of the story, related to me by an informant of Ait Sliman, it does illustrate one of the many roles that sultans played in the life of the tribes. It also shows the tribesmen's own view of their history. Both written and oral history indicate that the Ait Ndhir clans were already localized in their territories prior to the reign of Mawlay Hassan, but Berbers tend to peg all remembered events from their past onto the reign of the few really famous sultans, thus collapsing time.

back on the Omnaṣf division, each having to respect its position on one or the other side of the dual arrangement. However, if war was with a stranger, outside the tribe, the Omnaṣf ceased to operate. In other words, the upper limits of the thamunt was the tribe itself, and alliances never extended beyond the taqbilt. But it would be too easy to assume that this dualism was a permanent structure which functioned all the time. What seems to have happened was this: two or three powerful clans, always ranged on the opposite sides of the Omnaṣf, would compete for the leadership of the confederation; the other less powerful ones would be drawn into their orbits and ranged themselves on one side or the other depending on the nature of the issues and their range. For example, informants would always place the Iqeddaren versus the Harzallah and the Bourzouine versus the Naʻaman (these tribes had a reputation for being strong and belligerent); they would hesitate about the rest of tition. They would informants giving different versions of the repartition. They would usually conclude by adding that there was nothing sacred or permanent about these alliances, and that they tended to change with the intra-tribal wars.

An informant gave the following story of a recent intra-tribal war (circa 1905): "Aits Naʻaman and Iqeddaren were moving out in spring to their summer pastures. They were on the march near Sidi Aissa [on the road to Ifran], when one of the mounted Naʻamanis began to make indecent advances to a woman of the Iqeddaren. Her husband saw him and told him to leave her alone. The Naʻamani persisted and the husband became angry and shot him. This eventually grew into a fight that involved the whole tribe."

A rare eyewitness account of such an intra-tribal war was reported by Segonzac and the following lengthy quote from his book illustrates the nature of these engagements. The cortége of the sharif (with whom Segonzac was travelling) had just arrived among the Ait Naʻaman when

> ... suddenly, we heard an alarm and a volley of shots. The haiks[23] of the recall wave in the wind at the hilltops, the riders jump on their horses and gallop off.... The clan has been attacked by the Ait Iqeddaren. We are the involuntary pretext for the attack. The Ait Naʻaman had led our animals and us into the territory of the Iqeddaren. The latter, ignorant of the presence of the *sharif*, charged toward us, a skirmish resulted, shots were exchanged, the alert was founded ... thus begin battles among the tribe (Segonzac, 1903:108).

[23] A *haik* is a white, sheet-like garment that women wear when they are travelling or at souks. It is also known as *izar*.

Segonzac adds that despite the fighting, the casualty rate is usually very low and he attributes this to two reasons: the ammunition which the Berbers obtain as contraband from the Spanish is usually of poor quality; and their objective is not to kill their adversary.

> He [the Ndhiri] would like to wound seriously his adversary without killing him. He kills only when blind with fury since the law of the war demands that each death must be avenged by another death. No peace is possible between the clans whose casualties are unequal (Segonzac, 1903:110).

If the warring clans decided to suspend the hostilities for a certain time, they concluded a truce, *hana*. This truce could last anywhere from 24 hours to a year. For the duration of the truce, the members of the two clans would avoid one another, since in theory a state of war still existed between them. Segonzac stayed among the Ait Ndhir long enough for the sharif to conclude such a truce between the two parties. Again the procedure for the truce and the attitudes of participants are best described in Segonzac's own words:

> The enemy camp [Ait Iqeddaren] has just learned of the presence of the *sharif* in their midst and has realized their sacriligious error of having fired on him. Envoys leave the other camp and come to implore his pardon and to discuss the conditions of a truce.... Mawlay Ali [the *Sharif*] receives the envoys and suggests an agreement.... Our presence results in the acceptance of a truce for four months, after which the hostilities will no doubt resume (Segonzac, 1903:112-113).

Without casting any doubts on the prestige or the ability of the sharif or on the tenacity of Segonzac, one is tempted to add that since the truce was concluded in the month of May, it was no doubt prompted by the approaching harvest as much as by the above stated reasons.

When fighting each other, the clan suffering the most casualties usually asked for aman or hana (peace). As soon as the fighting was stopped, the amghars involved went out and counted the casualties on both sides. The clan with the most dead had to be compensated by the victors. Blood money (diyya) was paid to the relatives of those who were killed in much the same way as for an intra-clan murder. I am of the opinion that all intra-tribal fighting partook more of the nature of a feud, than a war. In other words, such fighting was viewed as blood revenge within a political community rather than as armed conflict between autonomous political communities. In this context, the necessity to settle the credit-debit balance of human life through the diyya becomes clear. Only in this way could clans prevent the perpetuation of a state of feud, which would be intolerable because it would interfere with the necessary, automatic coalescing of the confederation in the likelihood of an attack by an outsider. The confederation, after all, was nothing more than a pattern of military organization (formation guerrière) that managed to accommodate internal differences in the face of external threats.

There was a gain in interclan fighting, albeit a subtle one. The clan that inflicted more casualties and forced its antagonist to ask for peace gained moral credit among the totality of the Ait Ndhir, prestige and status that could be summoned when the victorious clan desired to initiate an alliance, exploit a certain pasture, or challenge a qaid. The financial loss suffered in paying the diyya was more than compensated for in terms of prestige and persuasive force within the confederation.

PACTS OF BROTHERHOOD AND PROTECTION

Despite the ephemeral nature of the thamunts among the Ait Ndhir, they did function to extend the sphere of mutual protection and cooperation among the different individuals and segments of the society. A special kind of alliance was that of the *taymat* (from Berber *aytma*: brothers). The taymat was a voluntary pact of friendship between two individuals that need not involve their respective families. Taymat implied such mutual assistance and economic cooperation as breeding sheep and aiding in harvest, and the exchange of hospitality and women in marriage. The ceremony sealing the pact involved the sharing of food but no sacrifice, although the participants often recited the *fatiha* (the first chapter of the Quran) together in order to lend solemnity to the occasion.

The Amur

There were several kinds of the *amur*, or pacts of protection (more generally known among tribes by its Arabic name, *mezraq*). One was a "secular" contract drawn up between two individuals, one of whom was usually a stranger to the tribe. In return for a sum of money, a tribesman agreed to escort the stranger, who might be a traveller in the area or an itinerant merchant, through the territory of the clan. The money exchanged was called *tazettat*, the toll fee. In general, those who acted as protectors had to be important and respected men in their clans in order for their group "to stand in their back," should any trouble occur. The Ait Ndhir, along with the other tribes that lived along major trade routes, such as the Ait Sidi Ali of the Seghrouchen and the Ait Youssi, must have derived a substantial income from this *amur n tazeṭṭat*. They, therefore, had to defend their reputation as responsible protectors, as the following story illustrates.

> One day, a caravan came out of the qasba of Al Hajeb and placed itself in the amur of a man from the Ait Naʻaman. The fee was 6 ryals. As the caravan was going through the territory of Ait Naʻaman, a man from the Harzallah came up to it and demanded money. When they refused to pay him, he fired on the caravan. The Naʻamani ran to his douar and shouted, "Oh my people, come and help me, the *ʻar* has touched me [meaning I was shamed]." And the Ait Naʻaman took their guns and fought the Harzallah. Thirty-six people were left dead after the battle.

Groups as well as individuals could grant amur. The jmaʻa of a douar, clan, or tribe would guarantee the safety of a market pitched on its territory; ikhataren and amghar saw to it that no thefts or fights took place in the market place. Protection was also given to shurfa and other dignitaries travelling in the area. In all these cases, no sacrifice was involved; the pledge was given verbally in front of witnesses.

Another, more solemn and personal amur pact involved no exchange of money. This amur was always contracted between two individuals of unequal status, and was in the nature of a patron-client relationship. This amur was also known among some Ndhiris by the Arabic term, *khuwa*, meaning brotherhood.

> A stranger [who could be a member of the tribe] desiring to reside for a time in a particular douar, would inquire about a strong and respected *akhatar* [elder] of the community. He would then take a sheep and sacrifice it in front of the akhatar's tent declaring loudly, "I wish to become your amur" and the akhatar would say, *"mrhbannek"* [I welcome you]. The man then lived near his akhatar's tent and he was referred to as "the man who is protected by so and so." If he was insulted or robbed, the akhatar had to avenge him [the patron also claimed his blood money]. If the man [patron] failed in this, he lost face [status] in the community. People would build a stone tomb [actually pile stones] at the cross road and all the passers-by would throw a stone at it, saying, "This is the tomb of so and so who does not keep his amur." It is as if the man were dead.

Patrons were always men who were well off and influential in their douar, for only then would their word be "worth something," i.e., in terms of the force they could muster to back them up. For despite the principle of the equality of all males of the lineage, a strong influential male is actually worth more since in effect he "represents" more males.

The Alliance of the Taḍa

An important kind of alliance was the *taḍa*.[24] The Ndhiris differentiate two kinds of taḍas (*taḍa biljouj*): the inner (*dakhlaniya*) and the upper (*foqaniya*). The taḍa dakhlaniya was a freely contracted alliance between two rifs or two douars, not necessarily of the same taqbilt.

> When these decided to make a taḍa, they took their tents and pitched them together on high ground, so everyone could see. Then they took the slippers of all the men who wanted to enter this taḍa and threw them in the middle of the gathering, mixing them up. Each man from one group [only] retrieved his slipper with a mate from the other group's slippers. They then found the owner of the mate and the two men embraced and called each other "Ait ou taḍa." Afterwards they sat and shared a meal together. This taḍa was very important and lasted from one child to the next [meaning from one generation to the next]. If anyone broke the rules of the taḍa, God punished them.

The taḍa was taken very seriously by the participants. It implied mutual aid and trust and guaranteed entree and hospitality among the tigemmis.

Old men in the tribe still use the term *ou'taḍa* to identify trusted friends of their douar. One day, I was taken to an old man, a former amghar, for an interview. The man who introduced me was a nephew of the amghar, and I was presented as a "good friend and a respectable woman." As I was sitting interviewing the old man, another elder came and joined us. This one wanted to know who I was, and his friend, my informant, turned to him and said, "This woman is a friend of us, since she is the ou'taḍa of my nephew Idriss."

The second taḍa, the *taḍa foqaniya*, was an alliance concluded between two clans. In this case, the jma'as involved met in a tent, sacrificed their sheep, and feasted one another. "Then they gave their word to each other, preferably in the presence of a sharif. This taḍa also lasted till the death of all the participants. For example, we the Iqeddaren, have a taḍa with the Ait Hammad that is still going on today, and it will end only when my friends and I die" (see Appendix III).[25] Clans joined in taḍa were forbidden to intermarry for the duration of the taḍa. The major function of this

---

[24] The verb *taḍ* means "to nurse" in Tamazight and Ait Ndhiris say that at one time in their past, certain taḍas involved ceremonies of colactation. The participants exchanged milk that was obtained from nursing mothers of the respective groups involved (see G. Marcy 1936:957-973).

[25] My informant was a very old man who insisted that this taḍa was still operative today, much to the disbelief and amusement of the young tribesmen who were present.

alliance was the regulation of theft and adultery, violations of which were believed to be punished automatically through supernatural sanctions (see Appendix IV). However, the taḍa did not impose the obligation of mutual assistance in intra-tribal war. When asked about the contradictions and possible strains resulting from such an omission, an informant said, "It is like this; we, the Iqeddaren, have a taḍa with Ait Hammad, but we fall on opposite sides of the Omnaṣf. Now, if we find ourselves in a fight, we will try to avoid shooting at each other. We will send word that our men will be behind such and such a rock and the Hammad will stay away from that place. If any one of them becomes our prisoner, or is wounded, we treat him well and send him to his people." Even though, in theory, the taḍas were binding from one generation to the next, there seem to have been ways of revoking them. Informants said that if the ou'taḍa found themselves breaking too many of the rules, such as allowing many cows to wander over boundaries, or abducting women from the ou'taḍa clan, then the ikhataren might decide to suspend their taḍa. Otherwise they would run the risk of incurring supernatural wrath. But this must have occurred very rarely, for I was unable to find anyone who could describe such a revocation ceremony.

VIOLENCE AND THE MORAL ORDER

The surest measure of the integration of the individual into the clan among the Ait Ndhir was his participation in the payment of the diyya or blood money. In fact, among the Ndhiris it seems to have been the only shared group activity and the most expressive manifestation of lineage membership. It constituted the decisive criterion, not only for acquiring lineage membership but also for losing it. But what is significant about the functioning of the diyya among the Ait Ndhir is that its rate was constant regardless of the agnatic distance of the two persons involved.[26] Thus the diyya was the same if a tribesman killed his cousin, a Ndhiri from a nearby douar, a Ndhiri from another clan, or even a Mguildi. Moreover, "damage" was compensated even within the smallest segment, i.e. the nuclear family. This procedure plays havoc with the notion of the irreducibility of the minimal lineage and renders the Ait Ndhir essentially a collection of individuals fitted loosely into different groups whose form and contour varied with situations.

[26] Among Arab tribes in general, and Iraqi ones in particular, the amount of the diyya is highest for the murder of cousins and decreases proportionately with the increase of kinship distance between agnates. Also, a father, unless insane, is responsible to no one if he kills his son, whereas a son committing patricide is banished from the tribe (see F. M. Al-Fira'un, 1941).

> Pour les raisons que nous ne dirons pas, un homme tue sa mère; le frère ou le père de la victime réclame le prix de sang. Le fils refuse de verser la "dia" alléguant que le sang versé étant celui de sa mère; il n'a dédommager qui ce soit. Le litage est porté devant un arbitre, qui applique *l'izref*. En l'occurance, ... le fils est tenu de payer une *dia* de femme, mais le frère ou le père de la victime doit restituer la dot qu'il atouchée lors du mariage de la femme. La criminel verse donc une *dia* diminuée de la dot de sa mère (Abes, 1918:56).

British ethnologists, in general, have deemed it necessary to posit peace and a state of equilibrium as required conditions for the pursuit of organized social life. Corporate existence was seen to be incompatible with a permanent state of feud and general anarchy. But, as Jeanne Favret (1968) has pointed out, violence is endemic to the organized life of the Berber tribes (and Arab tribes, for that matter). Among the Ant Ndhir there were no mechanisms for containing or reducing violence automatically. When conflict broke out in a douar, the jma'a would meet and attempt to resolve the differences through persuasion. Failing that, they would call on the *ahechamen* (arbitrators) who then proceeded to determine the guilt and recommend the form and amount of compensation. In all of this, the amasai had to be present for it was his duty to see to it that the judgment was executed. All murders were conceived of in credit and debit terms (*hada kullu dein*). Any willfully inflicted death opened an account between the segments involved, an account that had to be paid up through the diyya for only when this was done would all the obligations be discharged and the situation brought back to "normal." Each ighs had its own izref that specified the diyya in terms of the injuries sustained.[27] In the case of a murder, an effort was always made by the jma'a to locate the individual responsible and make him pay the full amount of the blood money. If he were incapable of doing so, he was required to pay ¼ of it and the other ¾ was divided equally among all the takhamats of his douar, his own included. Should a man be accused of a crime and there were no witnesses, he could be asked to produce a number of co-jurors (their number varied with the nature of the derelict) known as *imagilla*, who were willing to swear to his innocence. Normally, but not necessarily, these co-jurors would be agnates of the accused. Failing to round up the necessary number of co-jurors from his own douar, the accused would sacrifice a sheep in front of the tent of any man and place the "stranger" under obligation of serving as his co-juror. The co-jurors would make

---

[27] In April of 1918, the French gathered all the jma'as of the Ait Ndhir in a general meeting that resulted in a standardized and codified izref for the whole tribe (see Marcy, 1949:481-511).

SOCIOPOLITICAL ORGANIZATION 77

certain that the man was innocent before they undertook the collective oath. Giving false testimony was believed to expose the man to the risk of suffering supernatural punishment as well as being liable for the payment of part of the compensation.

> Collective oath (*tagellat*) is a legal decision procedure. It is a method for determining the truth or falsity of an accusation, and thereby terminating (at any rate, in theory) the dispute occasioned by that accusation. It is a method that invokes supernatural sanctions. It requires that a number of "co-jurors" (*imagellan*) testify, in a fixed order, and in a holy place, that the accusation is false. If they refuse to do so or fail to do so or make a slip when doing so, the accusation is held to be established and the accused party is obliged to make to the injured party the reparation foreseen by customary law for the offense in question . . . the co-jurors are of course not witnesses; it is not supposed that they necessarily or indeed generally have access to knowledge concerning whether the alleged culprit is or is not guilty. It is merely supposed that they know his general character, or are willing to vouch for his conduct, and are prepared to share the penalties imposed by mundane, or extra-mundane forces in punishment for their testimony, should it be false (Gellner, 1969:106).[28]

In this manner, the institution of the collective oath functioned to draw a number of people into an unresolved conflict, people who developed a stake in a quick and "honorable" settlement of the conflict. In the absence of specialized agencies, the pressure of public opinion saw to it that the moral order of the society was not violated and that conflicts were quickly resolved.

THE SOCIAL ORDER OF THE AIT NDHIR: CONCLUDING REMARKS

It should be clear from the above that it is both arbitrary and unrewarding to conceive of the sociopolitical system of the Ait Ndhir in exclusively segmentary or alliance terms. A more realistic interpretation would be derived if one were to view the social order in terms of a dynamic interplay of the two models. An alliance could reinforce the lineage, contradict it, or even replace it altogether. Many times, a segment had to make a choice between respecting lineage solidarity or upholding its own political expediency. This was obvious from the reaction of the tribe to the French in-

---

[28] For a general discussion of the role and significance of the collective oath in the segmentary system of the Berbers, see Gellner, 1969:104-110. Gellner mentions the story of the French officers "who had so completely misunderstood the institution of the collective oath that they wished to penalize co-jurors for 'bearing false witness.' Though a misunderstanding indeed, its effect was that they blasphemously usurped a function of the deity. On this occasion, vengeance was not the Lord's but the District Officer's."

vasion, when "cousins" joined different factions and started to raid one another. Therefore, one may safely say that, although agnatic segmentation, or its ideology in this case, defined broadly the spheres of political cooperation and the level at which conflict was to be evaluated and dealt with, it did not determine them. The function of the different alliances was to provide alternatives in the case of the failure of lineage cohesion.

In conclusion, the "order" of this society proves difficult to describe. It is riddled with contradictions, general amorphousness, and overlapping units which were dynamic and can only be defined adequately in terms of outside events which were often negative in nature—a feud, a raid, or a war. The segments did not come together along any discernable structural lines for weddings, religious ceremonies, or economic activities. As with all tribal societies, the social organization among the Ait Ndhir was idealized in terms of the kinship system and its various extensions, of which the ighs was the most important since it was the level at which kinship and political spheres met. On the other hand, one must not exaggerate the role of "tribalism" in the daily life of the individual Ndhiri, who seemed to have retained a remarkable freedom in interpreting and manipulating his sociopolitical universe.

V

THE DYNAMICS OF TRADITIONAL LAND TENURE AND TRIBAL ORGANIZATION

WITH the establishment of the Protectorate the French directed their attention to the delineation and regulation of the Moroccan land ownership system and the assessment of procedures for a large-scale colonization of land. Protectorate jurists proceeded to study and interpret the native land tenure system and to translate it into meaningful categories for the Political Officers who were charged with the implementation of the land colonization program. This chapter examines the nature of traditional land tenure, specifically in terms of its relationship to tribal groups; Chapter VI will deal with the impact of the French land colonization program on the Ait Ndhir.

THE MAKHZAN LAND TENURE SYSTEM

A study of the nature of Moroccan tribalism is clearly no place for a comprehensive discussion of so large and complex a subject as the pre-Protectorate Moroccan land categories. However, a presentation of the major features of traditional land tenure and land use is necessary for the understanding and proper evaluation of subsequent intervention by the French. Moreover, a knowledge of the traditional legal and administrative approach to land and the human groups that occupied it is crucial for a valid appreciation of makhzan-tribal interaction in Morocco. It is obvious that tribes were, to a large extent, defined in terms of their political relationship to the government; thus one may say that there were guish tribes, *naiba*, *taraf*, and *siba* tribes. Moreover, the political status of the human group was often extended to the legal status of the land occupied by the group. Since the political status of a tribe varied with time as a function of dynamic changes, the legal status of tribal land was rarely, if ever, clearly defined or resolved. Furthermore, despite subsequent efforts of the French to define and delimit tribal land ownership and use in Morocco, the situation is far from settled even today.

In order to understand the nature of the indigenous land system which the French found in operation upon their arrival in Morocco, it is necessary to refer back to the classic Arab-Islamic concepts of land and land ownership. Morocco never came under the Ottoman domination, and hence the land system that prevailed represented a local modification of the medieval Islamic system that was codified, elaborated, and explained by the Abbasid jurist, 'Ali Al-Mawardi in his book, *Al-ahkam al-Sultaniya* (1960:125-140). A general working scheme based on Al-Mawardi's work and avoiding the contentions and controversies of the different schools of Islamic jurisprudence, is presented below.[1]

According to the classical Islamic view, the world is divided into two domains: the area of Islam, *dar al-Islam*, and the area of war, *dar al-harb*. That of war is inhabited by the enemy who, once subjugated, may be either killed or subjected to taxation. Dar al-Islam is divided into three major divisions:

(1) Al-Haram, Mekka, and its immediate environs;
(2) Al-Hijaz;
(3) Other territories.

The "other territories" are in turn divided into three categories: territories whose inhabitants voluntarily converted to Islam, territories that were conquered by force, *'unwa*, and territories whose inhabitants capitulated through treaty, *sulha*. If the inhabitants of the capitulated territories chose to live as non-Moslems, they had to pay the *jizya*, a poll tax in recognition of their tributary status. However, if they chose to convert to Islam, they, like other Moslems, were liable for religious taxes only, the *zakat* and *'ashur*. The zakat was a 2.5 percent property tax (on capital and/or animals) while the 'ashur was a 10 percent income tax on all revenue (including the harvest).

If the inhabitants of an area did not capitulate, but were conquered by force, or if they abandoned their territory and fled in the face of the Moslem conqueror, their land was sequestered, *waqf* to the Moslem community *umma*, and they were liable to the payment of the land tax, *kharaj*. The waqf, in one of its many meanings,

---

[1] Moroccan jurists follow the Malki school of jurisprudence; their basic reference book is Sidi Khalil's *Al-Mukhtasar*.

refers to state land which, on being conquered, becomes the property of the whole Moslem community. However, the usufruct of the land remained in the hands of the original owners on their payment of the kharaj.[2]

The kharaj was an agricultural tax levied on the harvest; its rate varied with the nature of the crop and the soil. It could be calculated either in terms of the yield or the amount of land cultivated. The kharaj, which was paid in cash or kind, formed one of the principal sources of revenue of the Moslem community. Moslem jurists interpreted it to mean the rent paid by the inhabitants in return for their use of the land that really belonged to the community as a whole. The Sultan, in his role of imam, or head of the religious community, was charged with the administration of this property. He was given the right of supervision, *raqaba*.[3] Sultans were to use the kharaj revenues for the benefit of the whole community, to pay troops, construct mosques, and dig canals. The actual use of the property remained with the occupants who, in theory, had no right to sell or pledge the land.

Moroccan sultans extended the status of kharaj to all of Morocco declaring the whole country to be waqf of the community of which they were the leaders.[4] The application of the kharaj to all of Morocco resulted from a protracted legal debate by early Moroccan jurists over the nature of the Islamization of the country. To consider all of Morocco as liable to tax meant that there was no spontaneous conversion to Islam, but an overall conquest.[5]

GUISH AND NAIBA TRIBES

In 1188, Sultan Ya'qoub Al-Mansour (1184-1199) established several Arab tribes in the western region of Morocco where the original population was reduced as a result of the Berghouatta wars

---

[2]Islamic law recognizes private property, mulk, where individual owner has the rights of "usus, fructus, and abusus." The vivication of a dead land, *mawat*, for a consecutive number of years, usually 10, conferred on the cultivator the rights of private ownership.

[3]The right of supervision, *raqaba*, was later translated by the French jurists as "droit éminent."

[4]The Almohad sultans were the first to consider all of Morocco as conquered territory and the inhabitants as liable to the payment of kharaj. They based their claim on the fact that they were bringing real Islam to a population that had reverted to paganism. The founder of the dynasty, Mahdi ben Toumert (1078(?)-1128), preached the jihad against all other tribes, who were considered infidels. In fact most Moroccan dynasties emerged on the coattails of religious movements; all opposed were considered heretics. It is likely, therefore, that whole categories of liabilities had to be continually redefined.

[5]The debate about the nature of the original Islamization of the country and a related one regarding the nature of the Moroccan caliphate are far from settled even today. Some modern native historians are reexamining these issues as they rewrite their history (see Lahbabi, 1958).

and the many contingents sent to fight in Spain. Al-Mansour used these tribes as his militia to subdue the population and to aid him in the establishment of a regular administrative system that came to be known as the makhzan. These tribes were designated guish tribes; in time this practice became institutionalized and the guish tribes formed the military arm of the sultanate. They were charged with fighting the enemy at the frontiers and with putting down internal tribal rebellions.[6]

The alliance of the dynasties with the different tribes formed one of the most distinctive traits of the political history of Morocco. The Merinids were supported by the Arab Hilalian tribes of Khlot and Sefian and the Ma'aqil Chabanat. The Merinids were believed to be the first dynasty to repay the military service of the tribes by granting them usufructuary rights on domain land and exempting them from the land tax.[7] Sultans retained the right of *naql*, displacement of the group, for in theory the guish were permanently mobilized groups at the beck and call of sultans.

During the sixteenth century, the Sa'adis came to power aided by the Ma'aqil tribes of the Sus and the Sahara. The Sa'adi sultans proceeded to strike from the guish register the names of the Hilalian tribes that had championed the preceding Watassi dynasty and obliged them to pay the kharaj. However, this particular tax came to be called the naiba tax, from the Arabic word *naba*, to replace, referring to the fact that the military function of the Hilalian was now replaced by other tribes. The term naiba was then extended to refer to all tribes that paid the land tax and whose status was not that of guish to the dynasty.[8]

The naiba tax, called *farḍa*, was never standardized; it depended on the whim and need of individual sultans. A sum was levied on a tribe by the Sultan's agent, the qaid. This sum was then collected from the individual households by the jma'a. The arbitrary nature of the tax and the fact that sultans often ordered naiba tribes to furnish auxilliary troops in time reduced these tribes to a dependent status. It should be added that these tribes, just as the guish, were considered to hold usufructuary rights to their land.

[6] Morocco had no professional army until the second half of the nineteenth century when Sultan Abderrahman (1822-1859) began an army which later developed into a permanent one with professional soldiers, 'askar.

[7] For the relationship of the Merinid and Sa'adi dynasties with the Hilalian and Ma'aquil tribes, see H. Terrasse (1950, II:240-250).

[8] This explanation of the origin of the naiba tribes does not include the pejorative meaning of the term "naiba" to such groups as the Ait Ndhir who tend to equate it with an inferior and servile status. According to the Ait Ndhir the naiba tribes were too weak to be independent and had no choice but to place themselves under the protection of the dynasty.

The institution of the guish was developed and systematized by the early Alawi sultans, notably Mawlay Ismael who created three new guish tribes: the Bouakher, Oudaya, and the Tadla.[9] In reality, the majority of the guish tribes were amalgams of several distinct segments that were administratively grouped together under the command of a Sultan-appointed leader called the Pasha of the guish. The motivations that prompted these groups to ally themselves to the dynasty varied: some, like Oulad el Hajj of the Sais plain south of Meknes, referred to themselves as "the belt of Mawlay Idriss,"[10] thus identifying ideologically with Idrissi dynasties. Others, such as the Cherarga, or the Ait Ayash, represented the remnants of once powerful groups that were defeated and relocated piecemeal on hostile territory by sultans. These groups subsequently had little alternative but to ally themselves to the makhzan.[11]

Guish Status and the Land

As mentioned earlier, the Sa'adi sultans were the first to distinguish between the guish and naiba status and to grant the former special concessions in land. The sultans ceded a territory to the guish tribe collectively under a special category called *manfa'a*. The individual tribesmen, soldiers-laborers (called *mkhaznis*), received their share of this territory in individual usufruct known as *inti fa'*. The plots were divided and distributed by the Pasha of the tribe who registered each individual and his allotted piece in a special book called *diwan al-guish*. Among some guish tribes, the plots were rotated periodically. The right to individual usufruct had to be renewed on the death of the original recipient; only the male heirs were eligible.

Mawlay Ismael imposed a military hierarchical organization on the tribal one. Each guish tribe was divided (in principle) into sections of 1000 adult males each called *reha*, under the command of *qaid er reha*. These, in turn, were subdivided into units that were made up of four *reba'a* sections under the leadership of one

---

[9] The guish tribes proper of the Alawi dynasty were: Bouakher, Oudaya, Cherarda, Cherarga, Mjatt, Ait Ayash, Ait Rob'a, and Ymmour. The account of the guish is based primarily on Terrasse I (1949); II (1950) LeCoz (1965:1-35) and Michaux-Bellaire (1911: 74-89).

[10] Mawlay Idriss was the founder of the first Islamic dynasty in Morocco.

[11] A Ndhiri informant said, "You could look at it this way: the guish tribes were the leff of the Sultanate." The Cherarga (or Easterners) were a composite group made up of several Arab-speaking tribal segments that were driven off Tlemcen and Oujda by the Ottomans. Mawlay al-Rachid (1666-1672) had them installed near Fez, made them his guish and added to them some Berber speaking groups such as Houara and Beni Snous.

moqaddam who was the liaison between the *jma'as* of the tribal villages and the military hierarchy.

As can be seen in Figure 9, guish tribes were strategically placed around the cities of Marrakesh, Meknes, Fez, and Tangier. The two exceptions were the Cherarga and Ait Rabaa. The Cherarga were stationed near the qasba of Sidi Kacem to guard the important military and commercial route through the valleys of Sebou and Rdom. The Ait Rabaa were placed near qasba Tadla and charged with blocking the expansion of the Berbers of the High Atlas.

Beginning in the late nineteenth century, the periodic division and rotation of land within the guish tribes, as well as their continual displacement, fell into neglect. The Pashas failed to keep their registers up to date or renew the land concessions. Tribesmen started to buy and sell the land as if it were private property, *mulk*; and it was passed to heirs and divided according to the *shari'a*.[12]

It should be emphasized that the term guish referred to the status of the group and not to the land, which was simply kharaj land given under the special concession of collective usufruct, manfa'a. The territorial base of guish tribes, as with all other tribes, varied with the strength of the group and its demography. Furthermore some tribes often alternated between guish and rebelliousness (Mjatt, Cherarga, Ymmour).

Under the Protectorate, guish tribes became the subject of special legislation and treatment and a whole new category of land was created, the *bled guish*, or "les biens *guichs*."

THE 'AZIB INSTITUTION

During the second half of the nineteenth century, a new trend in land ownership and land use became discernible in the Moroccan countryside. This development took the form of large-scale appropriation of land and the emergence of proto-feudal estates in rural areas. The trend crystallized in the institution of the *'azib*.[13]

The Alawi Sultans, in the course of the exercise of their right of sovereignty (and in abuse of their right of supervision, raqaba), placed large areas under the protection of individual shurfa, qaids,

---

[12] The de facto appropriation of guish land by qaids and tribesmen became widespread during the years 1904-1915. Much of this land was sold to Europeans; see Michaux-Bellaire (1913:316-400); also W. D. Schorger (1969:272-273).

[13] The 'azib was often known in the Gharb region as *qaria*. The origin, evolution, and impact of this form of land concession in Morocco has yet to be fully studied. Its origin is generally attributed to Mawlay Ismael who bestowed estates on shurfa in recognition of their services to the dynasty. For fragmentary data on 'azib, see Aubin (1904:459-470); Michaux-Bellaire (1908:23-89); and J. LeCoz (1964:294-307).

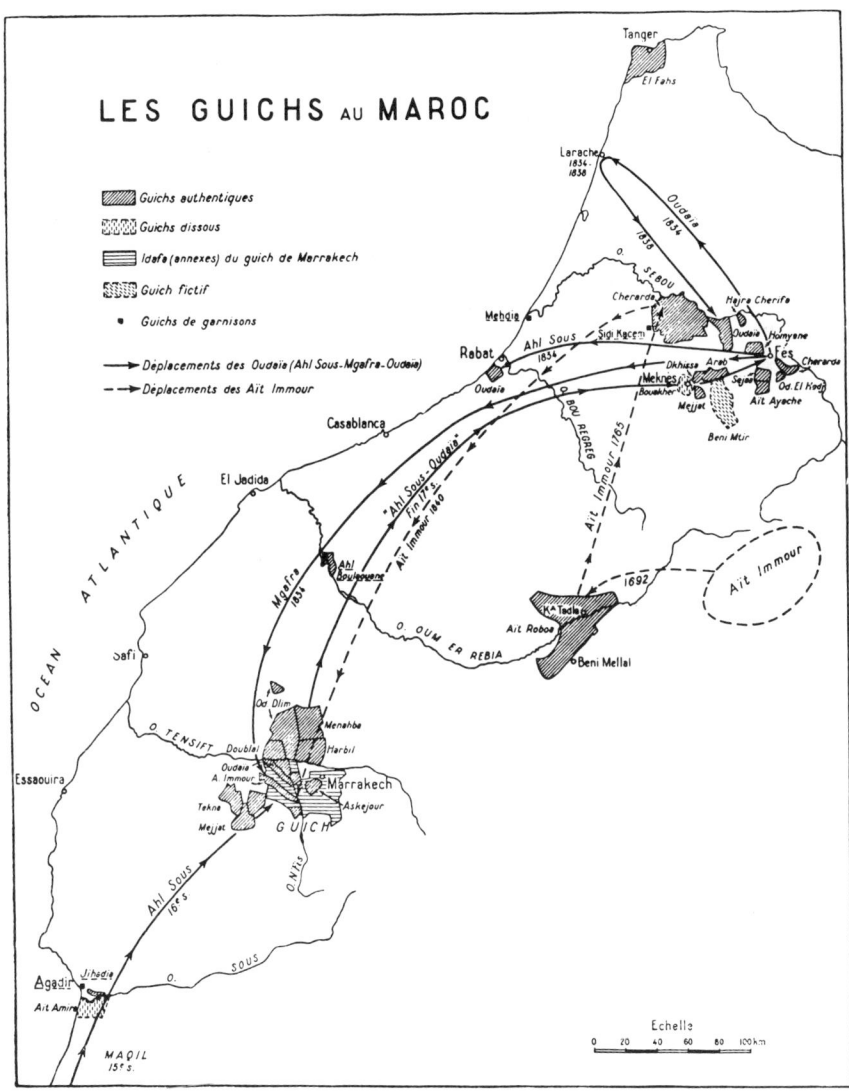

Fig. 9. Guish tribes of Morocco under the Alawi dynasty. From J. Le Coz, "tribus guichs au Maroc," Revue de Geographie du Maroc, no. 17, 1965, p. 2.

or zawiyas. This act was formalized by a sharifian edict, *dahir*, which stated that such and such a village or territory was given as 'azib to such and such a person. In effect, the person so designated came to rule over the area designated in very much the same way as the Sultan did over Morocco. The sharif, qaid, or zawiya received the religious taxes from the inhabitants of the 'azib as well as the hadiya, or gift.[14] Within the territory of the 'azib, the sharif ruled independently and his 'azib was considered inviolate even to the Sultan's troops. However, in order not to escape the authority of the Sultan completely, a deputy, *naqib*, was appointed for each 'azib and this deputy served as the liaison to the court.

On the death of the original recipient of the 'azib, his son had the choice of either leaving the 'azib or taking his father's place and staying. However, inheritance was not automatic, the heir being obliged to petition the Sultan for a renewal of the original concession. This process avoided the transformation of the 'azibs into permanent feudal estates and prevented the emergence of a stable landed aristocracy.[15]

The advantages to the shurfa and qaids of having 'azibs are obvious. However, there is evidence to indicate that the tribesmen and peasants themselves often asked the Sultan to make them part of an 'azib concession. Why would a Moroccan seek to contract such an obligation? Jacques Berque is of the opinion that the reasons for seeking this diffuse form of vassalage in Morocco stem from the natural veneration of shurfa as well as from a desire to escape the arbitrary exactions of the Sultan's agents and the nearby tribes. Within the 'azib, the peasant had to pay only the religious tax, the zakat (Berque, 1937:227-235).

To recapitulate, despite the novelty and significance of the 'azib as an alternative mode of socio-economic organization, its importance must not be exaggerated. In Morocco it remained fragile and the system of concessions, *iqta'*, never developed into an hereditary one.[16] The sultans used it to recompense individuals

---

[14] The *hadiya* was a manifestation of allegiance. Sultans received these gifts on ceremonial occasions from the different segments of the population, tribal chiefs, urban guilds, army units, etc.

[15] The 'azib has been defined as "village ou partie de village dont les habitants sont de père en fils concédés par le sultan à un chérif et sa descendance pour prélever sur eux l'aumône légale et toutes les relevances de soveraineté" (Michaux-Bellaire, 1908:72). But the exact nature of the relationship between the sharif or qaid and the peasants is not fully known and seems to have varied by regions. The 'azib institution represented a curious reversal of the European feudal model; in Morocco the aristocracy being mainly shurfa, were pacifists while their "vassals," the tribesmen, were all armed.

[16] For a recent and interesting analysis of the impact of the 'azib concession on the emergence of large personal domains in Morocco, see Lazarev (1968:99-135).

who served the dynasty. It must be emphasized that what was bestowed was not the land itself, but the privilege of collecting a fraction of the revenue derived from the land. The privilege remained precarious and dependent on the will and strength of the Sultan.

The Pax Gallica rendered the protection services of the shurfa and qaids obsolete and the 'azib institution atrophied. Nevertheless, in many areas, the 'azib concession was reinterpreted to mean joint patrimony (i.e., undivided mulk) of the shurfa families who proceeded to register the land in mulk. The tribal jma'as contested this in several areas. A case remains unsettled today where the Ait Bourzouin (Ait Ndhir) is contesting the ownership of some 150 hectares near Agourai which is claimed by a Regraga shurfa family of Meknes.[17]

TRIBAL TENURE: COLLECTIVE LAND

Land tenure in Morocco varied from the shari'a-regulated urban areas to distant areas in which customary usage qai'da prevailed, with many combinations in between. Among the tribes that were neither guish nor naiba, what the Ait Ndhir call the *taryazt* tribes, land ownership was collective.[18] The group considered itself the legitimate owner of the territory which it jointly defended. The original mode of acquisition was through conquest, *ḥaqq al-baroud* (the right of war, or the gun), and it was exploited in joint usufruct by all the males who were considered part of the tribe. Communal ownership and collective usufruct are adaptive mechanisms (solutions) in areas of Morocco characterized by a high degree of political instability and repeated contesting of resources. Within this context, the right to property is essentially reduced to the possibility of possessing, exploiting, and defending a given space. It was the politically organized group, the tribe, that was capable of maintaining and defending the communally owned property against rival claims.

Although collective property is not recognized by Moslem

[17] It seems that the shurfa often claimed and registered land as their private property regardless of the original form of concession; see LeCoz (1964:256-258); Vermeil, mem. de fin de stage controle civils, promotion de 1928, El Hajeb.

[18] It is difficult, if not impossible, to define the concept of collective land. Written law ignored it while customary definitions and usage varied over time and space. The Protectorate was the first to codify the system and define its contours. Article 1 of the dahir of April 27, 1919 stated that collective land is "terres de culture, ou de parcours, des tribus, des fractions, des douars ou des autres groupements indigènes, qui en jouissent à titre collectif, selon les modes traditionelles d'exploitation et d'usages." Indispensible for the study of collective land in Morocco are the following works: Tassoni (1928:100-124; 133-157); Amar (1914); and Milliot (1922).

law,[19] Moslem jurists appear to have accepted its existence and in fact Moselm judges, *qadis*, very often acted as arbitrators in litigation over collective land between jma'as of two clans.

Collective land is inalienable; it cannot be bought, sold, or transmitted through inheritance. Among the Berber tribes in general, each household obtained an equal share of the agricultural land; there was no distinction by need or size of extended family. Periodic reallotment and the exclusion of women prevented any one lineage from acquiring permanent rights to a specific piece of land and insured the integrity of the patrimony and the cohesion of the tribe.

Among the Ait Ndhir, once an individual left his tigemmi, he lost his right to a piece of land and the jma'a of the tigemmi could reassign his land. However, the rights were reactivated when the individual reestablished residence in his tigemmi. The procedures are derived from the fact that only the males who are present can share the responsibility in case of attack and insure the security of the territory. A stranger, once accepted by the jma'a, could be given a lot to cultivate; however, he would not be considered a full citizen until a certain number of years (usually between four and 10) had elapsed. Then, the individual could be formally accepted by the jma'a into the clan, and obtain the privileges of participation in the assembly.

Collective ownership must not be confused with joint property, a category recognized by Moslem law. In joint property each co-proprietor has a definite quota-part defined by the inheritance laws and which can be claimed upon division of the property. The concept of collective property, on the other hand, is a Durkheimian one: the whole group is the owner of the property, land being the manifestation of the solidarity of the group and the equality of its individual members. The representative assembly, jma'a, administers the property on behalf of the group. In principle, the jma'a should be composed of *all* the heads of household, since the notion of collective ownership is predicated on the absolute equality of all members.

Vexed by the predominance of collective tenure in rural Morocco, especially on the plain of the Gharb and among the dir tribes, French scholars began a protracted and confusing debate on the origins, evolution, and significance of collective ownership. The fact that tribal land was inalienable because it was communal

---

[19]Communally owned property is known all over the Arab Moslem world; in Algeria it is called *'arch*, in Tunis, *sabaga*, and in the Near East *masaha* or *musha'a*.

must have added a measure of urgency to the legal debate, since the pressure for colonization was apparent as early as 1917.

The debate regarding the nature of collective property was never resolved. One school of jurists, led by Surdon (1926), believed that the dominant property system in Morocco was the private one and that collective ownership resulted from long-term and persistent neglect to divide joint property. Michaux-Bellaire (1924:141-151), on the other hand, insisted that collective tenure was the norm and that private property in rural Morocco (outside the urban areas) represented a recent innovation in the original collective system. An inquiry made in the years 1921-25 revealed the predominance of collective ownership in the Gharb region (northwest Morocco) among the Beni Ahsen, Khlot, Chaouia, Zemrane, Zemmour, Zaer, and the Berber tribes of the dir region of the Middle Atlas. Le Coz, author of the most exhaustive socio-economic study on the Gharb region (1964), refers to collective tenure as the most distinctive feature of rural Morocco and adds

> Le charactère fondamental du *bled jma'â* consistait dans l'égalité potentielle des droits de tous les membres de la collectivité a jouisance de la terre. C'est un trait pour lequel était rendue impossible l'assimilation de la terre collective à la propriété indivise. Ne disposant que d'un droit actuel de jouisance et d'un droit éventuel de propriété, le collectiviste, à la différence du co-propriétaire indivise, ne pourait céder sa quotepart, ni transmettre à ses heritiers un biens déterminé, mais seulment des droit indéterminés, et en cas de partage chacun des collectivistes recevait un lot égal a celui des autres (283).

LAND TENURE AND LAND USE AMONG THE AIT NDHIR

Ait Ndhir informants all agree that prior to the French occupation, land belonged to the tribe and that the only possessions that an individual Ndhir had were his animals, his horse, and his gun. They add that all adult males had equal rights to the land: "We were all equal in war and we were all equal in land." Each of the 10 clans or ikhsan of the Ait Ndhir possessed a definite area, part of which was on the Sais plain. The area on the plain was divided among the douars or tigemmis that made up the clan. The jma'a of each of the douars was charged with dividing the agricultural land among the individual households (*takhamt*). The Ait Ndhir did not fight over land because of the available abundance of fertile land. Contested boundaries between two camp units were settled by the jma'as involved.

Collective ownership, by which only the jma'a possessed the

right to alienate land, and the political instability in the region discouraged the encroachment of city notables on tribal territory. The only people who owned private property on Ndhiri land were the shurfa. In 1915, the political officer in charge of the Ait Ndhir reported that only few hectares of the approximately 1,150,000 sq. km claimed by the tribe were mulk and that these all belonged to Arab shurfa from Meknes and Fez (Abes, 1918:54). All of these shurfa possessed written titles to their land.

Tribal informants claim that the land was originally given to the shurfa families by the different jmaʻas as *habous*.[20] However, it seems that these urban-based shurfa proceeded to register the land as if it was theirs in mulk.[21]

In addition to delineating the areas on the Sais plain for the use of each camping unit, tigemmi, the clan assembly set aside an area for the use of the clan chief amghar as reimbursement for the costs of hospitality and gifts to the shurfa or visiting dignitaries.

Apart from the cultivated land, all the other land of the clan (including the areas that were fallow) was left for the collective use of all clan members. Whenever the tribe was at war with the makhzan, it abandoned its cultivated territories and retired to the plateau; as things improved, they regained the plain and each tigemmi camped in its usual territory.

Under normal conditions, sons inherited rights of usufruct to the same lots cultivated by their father. The women held no right to land or any other property. Strangers could rent land from the jmaʻa, which collected a certain portion of the harvest in payment.

> Les ventes de terrain chez les Aith Ndhir sont relativement rares. Nous avons dit, en effet, que la tribu a en ce moment beaucoup de terre. Cependant, il y a des cultivateurs qui veulent étendue leur domaine et qui achètent non pas le sol qui est à la collectivité, mais l'usufruit de la propriété. Les échanges de terre sont aussi pratiqués. Ils ont été nécessités par le déplacement de tentes ou de douars entiers. Comme de juste, la propriétaire avantagé par l'obtention d'un lot plus fertile verse une indemnité fixée par les notables de la *jmaʻa* (Abes, 1918:63).

To sum up, it is likely that collective ownership, with its emphasis on the solidarity and equality of the group and the indivisi-

---

[20] Habous or waqf in this context means land over which the owner surrenders his rights of disposal with the stipulation that the yield is used for charitable purposes.

[21] Surdon summed up this consistent practice of the shurfa in this way: "Le caractére de la propriéte des *chorfa* ne saurait être que melk, car les *chorfa* ne s'incorporaient point au milieu desquelles ils vivaient... Le simple jouissance eut été peu goûteé par les *chorfa* lors de leurs installation dans la région et il n'est pas d'usage d'en user ainsi a leur égard, la simple jouissance étant réservée aux *tolbas* qui viennent en tribu pour servir d'écrivains publics" (Quoted in LeCoz, 1964:301). Surdon was supporting the claim of a tribal *jmaʻa* to land they had leased to shurfa.

bility of land, functioned to maintain the necessary cohesion of the Ait Ndhir in a politically unstable zone. It prevented the fragmentation of the tribe and at the same time served as a barrier to the intrusion of potential landlords from the nearby cities.

The mobile property, tents, and animals belonged to the males of the tribe. This fact rendered matrimonial alliance unimportant economically, because women provided no access to property. The only means to the acquisition of property were prolonged residence among the group and military service. Communal occupation of space insured a certain measure of equality within the tribe, and the management and exploitation of collective land forged a number of sodalities that insured group cohesion. Moreover, individual tigemmis, the basic socio-economic units, were embedded in a network of alliances, both economic and political. The extensive network of alliances and the lack of emphasis on agnatic affiliation, afforded the individual households and camp units a great measure of mobility that enabled them to seek refuge over a wide area. The institution of the sacrifice, tamghrost, whereby a stranger could gain temporary refuge and potential membership in any group, offered mobile protection to dispossessed individuals and their families.

THE AIT NDHIR TRIBE: AN ADAPTIVE INTERPRETATION

It is possible to interpret the history of rural Morocco, at least since the Sa'adi dynasty (sixteenth century), as a concentration of attempts by the makhzan to introduce a new type of society into the tribally organized countryside. The efforts of such sultans as Sidi Mohammad ben Abdalla (1757-90) and Mohammad ben Abderrahman (1859-73) surpassed the simple objective of gathering the tax. They attempted to settle the population and reorganize their socio-economic relationships and forms of property. This intervention took the form of settling tribes along hydraulic systems (such as the Tassouat canal near Marrakesh) or granting of tribal lands to qaids and zawiyas under the 'azib concession. But these attempts were not extensive or consistent enough to erode the tribal organization. Certainly in frontier zones, like the dir, they merely reinforced the tribal framework which served to organize individuals, distribute resources, and manage conflict.

Before going on to a consideration of the distortions introduced by the French, it may be worthwhile to summarize the mode of adaptation of rural groups in Morocco as exemplified by the Ait Ndhir.

The territory of the group was considered the joint patrimony of the whole tribe, *tamazirt n nun* (our land). The boundaries of this territorial base fluctuated with the changing balance of power among competing groups and with demographic pressures. The solidarity and cohesion of the group was less a result of their attachment to a common ancestor (which often was an ideological justification) than the common need to safeguard an ecological space considered necessary for the pursuit of their pastoral economy and extensive agriculture and to insure security against other groups of similar order of organization. At the base of this social organization was the extended household takhamt. These patriarchal, patrilineal families grouped into loosely structured patrilineages, ighs (often referred to in the diminutive form, *tighst*). The territorial expression of these segments was the camping unit, tigemmi.

The next level of organization was the ighs or the clan. The base of solidarity at this level was political rather than economic, dictated by the exigencies of common defense. The dimensions of the ighs were determined by the space necessary for the pursuit of the economic activity of all the constituent tigemmis. Among the Ait Ndhir, each ighs attempted to secure for itself complementary zones of the plateau and the plain that were necessary for the transhumant cycle.[22] Those clans that failed to combine adequate complementary space would forge special alliances insuring mutual accessibility to the different ecological zones as well as mutual defense of the vital space. This was the case among the Ait Ourtindi and Ait Boubidman. In all cases, the ighs represented the political framework within which group solidarity was a function of the common need to defend a vital agro-pastoral space.

Encircling the ighs, the tribe or taqbilt was the largest framework that delimited the physical and strategic unity of a number of clans. Within the framework of this organization, the territory of the taqbilt served more than simply an economic function; it was the strategic base for retreat and passage and a measure of the strength of the group. Small population, total integration of individual in the patriarchal family, and the instability of agricultural exploitation all encouraged communal ownership and collective usufruct.

In this shifting, evolving, complex universe of rural Morocco, the French imposed legal categories and social concepts derived from another cultural context and history. They succeeded in distorting and concealing the original reality.

---

[22] Among some groups of the Haouz of Marrakesh, it was found that the size of the clan (called *'adem*) corresponded closely to the labor forece necessary to dig up and maintain the irrigation canals in the area; see Lahlimi (1967:23-45).

VI

THE FRENCH PROTECTORATE AND LAND COLONIZATION

THIS chapter will consider briefly the legal mechanisms enacted by the French for the appropriation of the most fertile land in central Morocco. It concludes with an examination of the case of the Ait Ndhir.

FRENCH ORDER: THE LEGAL LABYRINTH

Articles 11 of the Convention of Madrid (1904) and 60 of the Act of Algeçiras (1906) made it possible for Europeans to acquire property in Morocco. In the years prior to the establishment of the Protectorate, Sultan Abd Al-Aziz limited the foreign acquisition of land to within a radius of 10 kilometers of all cities and to within a radius of eight kilometers of the ports. It quickly became evident to European speculators that most of the land around the cities was either habous or occupied by the guish. With the advent of the Protectorate, this technicality did not prevent wild speculation in and massive sale of indigenous property under circumstances that were far from legal. In fact, land speculation and sale reached such scandalous proportions that the government was forced to find means of preventing the wholesale dispossession of tribal groups.

The *dahir*[1] of November 1, 1912, stated that "les terres occupeès en collectivité par des tribus restront telles qu'elles sont et continueront a être régis par les anciens usages, sans pouvoire être vendues ou partagées" (Guillaume, 1960:19). Following this, a number of dahirs followed between the years 1914-1916. Some of these instructed the religious judges, qadis, to be careful in granting titles to newly divided tribal land and to guard specifically against the transfer of tribal property to qaids and other notables. The motives behind this policy were not all altruistic. French native officers

---

[1] A *dahir* or more correctly, *daheer*, is a royal edict issued under the seal of the Sultan.

believed that by disturbing the rural people least, they could maintain peace and order in the countryside allowing the army to pursue the conquest of the rest of Morocco.

It soon became clear that this admirable policy had to be modified. The massive influx of post-World War I immigrants from France, all hungry for land, obliged the Protectorate to seek means and ways of providing for the acquisition of land. The policy makers were caught between two contradictory aims: on the one hand, they wanted to "protect" the peasants and tribesmen and allow them to pursue their traditional life; on the other, they sought to reorganize them and confine them to a part of their land, making the remaining land available for colonization. A legislative solution was sought for this problem; the ultimate aim was to regulate the transfer of property and to make the collectively owned land areas available for sale. French jurists, working in collaboration with the political officers, produced a barrage of edicts, statutes, and books all pertaining to the classification and definition of the land ownership system in Morocco. Between the years 1919 and 1925, the thrust of the colonial effort was to define the exact status of guish and tribal land and to find the "legal" means of making both of these categories available for sale. One is spellbound by the erudition and time devoted to the construction of the elaborate legal facade whose aim and result was to defraud the Moroccans out of their best land. A concomitant result was the establishment of a cumbersome bureaucracy staffed with a large number of French civil servants.

It is interesting to follow here the change in French attitude and assessment of the Moroccan land tenure system. The earliest published works on the subject were primarily concerned with private property, mulk. They sought to prove its widespread existence in Morocco and sought to reconcile it with the makhzan's practice of arbitrary movement of whole populations, naql. Collective property was treated briefly and offhandedly so as to give the impression that it was an unimportant institution of marginal significance (see Salmon, 1904:146). This could also reflect the stage of French penetration which at this time was confined to the northern cities. But, following the military expansion of 1912, the significance and predominance of collective ownership became gradually evident to the French. The efforts of their jurists to define collective land ownership culminated in the dahir of April 27, 1919, which is still considered to be the charter for collectively owned land in Morocco. Its text has been and still is the subject of numerous books and articles and some of its provisions are subject to debate. Briefly, the major points of the edict were:

(1) Collective property was defined as land belonging to a douar, clan or tribe, to which the whole group has collective usufruct. The primary characteristics of this property were that it was inalienable, imprescriptible, and unseizable. However, a codicil was attached to the effect that the state had the right to acquire the collective land through simple expropriation if it (the State) deemed it necessary for the public interest.

(2) The jma'a was recognized officially but was limited to the assembly of the clan, ighs, from which several members were coopted to represent the whole tribe. The civil duties of the jma'a were set down in writing; members were to be elected for a period of three years. The jma'a could delegate its authority to a representative, naib who had to be approved by the qaid, himself appointed by the Sultan.

(3) The overall supervision and administration of the collective property was placed under the tutelage of the State, or more precisely of the Director of Native Affairs, (changed to Director of Political Affairs in 1936). A council was established to administer the land. The council was presided over by a French magistrate assisted by two notables for each tribe; the notables were appointed by the Grand Vizier. The council was given the authority to overrule the tribal jma'a.

The continuing pressure for land soon caused a number of modifications and new interpretations to be attached to the original 1919 dahir. Of major importance was the limiting of collective land to uncultivated land (*mawat*, or dead land, recognized by the shari'a). All cultivated land was to be treated as joint property; that is to say it was to be divided among the households of the tribal section in private ownership. A stipulation was attached to the new title that prohibited the sale of this newly acquired property for a period that ranged from five to 10 years.

The distinction between cultivated and pasture land was a highly artificial one, since among the majority of the tribes of the Gharb region and the foothills of the Middle Atlas Mountains land use is rotated and no distinction is made between agricultural and pasture areas.

Thus in a series of progressive legal maneuvers, the French crystallized a uniform land category which they called *bled jma'a*, incorporated it under the jurisdiction of the State, and limited it to the less fertile areas.

THE CASE OF THE AIT NDHIR: "UN GUICH FICTIF"

The Protectorate, after a number of tentative trials at managing the guish-owned land, decided to assign the administration of the land to the Services des Domaines. Guish tribes were considered to be simply in usufruct of land which in reality belonged to the public domain.[2] The land was treated exactly as if it were collective land with one major difference—the tribes were considered squatters on the territory which belonged to the Sultan.

The government proceeded then to cede its rights to part of the land to the old guish families (the military functions of the guish were usurped by the French army and the professional Moroccan army). The balance of the land was turned over by the Sultan to the French official colonization program. Official colonization consisted of dividing the land into large lots that ranged from 250 ha to 500 ha, each of which was given to a French family for a reduced price with the stipulation that they would live on it and cultivate it "scientifically."

In reality, the concept of bled guish was of the same order as that of bled jma'a, an elaborate legal maneuver whose aim was to make available for the French immigrants some of the choicest land in central Morocco. The truth of the above statement is evident in the cases of the Bouakher and the Ait Ndhir.

The Bouakher was an authentic guish tribe in the service of the Alawi dynasty. It was formed in Marrakesh by Mawlay Ismael around a nucleus of an elite black guard established earlier by the Sultan Ahmad Al-Mansour (1578-1603). After a turbulent history of displacement, the Bouakher were installed to the west of Meknes. This proximity to the urban center meant that they were under the direct surveillance of the Sultan which provided them with a measure of political stability. In time, their guish status fell into disuse and the periodic redistribution of their land ceased to operate. During the first decade of the twentieth century, a large part of the Bouakher land was sold to Europeans and urban notables.

In 1916, the Protectorate identified the Bouakher as a guish tribe and delimited their territory to 17,000 ha. However, on closer inspection, it was found that a large number of Europeans (including Frenchmen, Italians, and some Spaniards) held title to about

---

[2]Houdas, the first translator of Al-Ufrani's book, *Nuzhat al Hadi fi Tarikh Alqarn Alhadi*, rendered the term *Beit al mal* as "le domain public de sultan." This was later equated by French jurists with public domain, a category with definite connotation in French law that is alien to the original meaning of *Beit al mal*, or the public treasury where the money was to be used for welfare of the whole Moslem community and Sultan was simply an administrator. Public domain was taken in Morocco to mean makhzan land, or crown land.

half of the area. To insist on the guish status of the Bouakher would mean the eviction of all of the European landlords, whose holdings were scattered all over the territory. The Protectorate then decided to abrogate the tribe's guish status and accept the de facto "illegal" land ownership that prevailed. The Bouakher were thus declared a non-guish tribe.

The inverse process occurred to the Ait Ndhir. The tribe was in possession of fertile land at the southern end of the Sais plain which was considered an excellent locale for mechanized cereaculture and viniculture. However, the tribally collective form of appropriation of the approximately 65,000 ha on the plain rendered this land inalienable and thus Frenchmen had no legal means of acquiring it. The authorities surmounted this difficulty by declaring the tribe guish.[3] This allowed the reclassification of Ndhiri land as douiam, or makhzan land and 20,000 ha of the most fertile land was then "legally" expropriated and turned over to official colonization. The rest of the land was then given to the tribe under the newly defined status of collective property, bled jma'a.[4] However, among those clans that owned extensive land on the plain, the Protectorate authorities divided cultivated land in mulk among the heads of households who registered. By 1921, approximately 2,058 had registered and these received 10 ha each. However, the allotted 10 ha were often made up of small, dispersed lots of uneven quality.[5]

The division of tribal land and its allocation to the Ait Ndhiris opened the way for private colonization of the tribal land. Ignorant of the value of land, and intimidated by the French army that was pressing the Ndhiris into corvées to clear roads and European farms, the tribesmen were quickly relieved of their newly acquired property.[6] Enterprising colons began by buying a few hectares that slowly formed a nucleus around which more and more land was accumulated. By 1924, 30,000 ha on the plain were owned by private colons, and such was the massive sale of land that a ministerial

---

[3] Some of the more liberal minded of the French administrators referred to the Ait Ndhir as "guich fictif." The expression appears in a report submitted by the controleur civil, Chief of the Meknes-Banlieu in 1931.

[4] For an example of the paternalistic attitude of the French Government and the procedure followed in land transactions with the Ait Ndhir see Appendix V.

[5] Ait Harzallah and Ait Ourtindi retained their land in collective ownership. They remained primarily pastoral and the bulk of their land was on plateau.

[6] Ndhiri informants said that many of them believed that the French would soon leave and things would go back to "normal." The sale of the land to Frenchmen was therefore seen as a clever device by the Ndhiris to gain some quick cash!

edict was issued prohibiting the Ait Ndhir from selling their property to Europeans for a period of 10 years.

This legal difficulty was circumvented; tribal intermediaries, often the newly installed qaids, would slowly group small parcels for a European colon and administer it for him. Many Ndhiri families were dispossessed of their land before they even took possession of it. In other cases, whole douars ended up landless. One such case involved the shurfa Boukilis who lived among the Ait Harzallah. In 1921, these shurfa constituted one tigemmi known as Kifan Bou Yousef; informants claim that it was made up of 28 households, all related. The French officers refused to acknowledge the Boukilis as shurfa and obliged the men to serve on the corvées that were organized by the French Army to clear roads, dig canals, clear colons' fields, etc. In order to escape this humiliating treatment, the jma'a of the douar decided not to register themselves and they gathered their tents and animals and retreated into the mountains. As a result, the whole douar was not included in the land distribution. In 1930, the tigemmi regrouped and was allowed to "squat" on the plateau on an area which was part of the collectively owned pasture land of the Harzallah. They are still "squatting" today. Some of the men served in the army and managed to accumulate some money with which they bought land nearby. The majority, however, are landless, and few manage to rent land from the jma'a of the Ait Harzallah. They sharecrop the land and give the jma'a one fourth of the harvest.[7]

Alarmed by the massive dispossession of land, some of the jma'as met and declared areas on the plain as collective property and held it in reserve for clan members. This was the case among the Ait Ouallal. Other factions, such as the Ait Boubidman were practically completely dispossessed.

In 1919, the clan of Ait Boubidman had a territory measuring approximately 14,000 ha.[8] This was divided among the four ikhsan that comprised a total of 21 tigemmi (see Fig. 10). In 1920, 3,039 ha were ceded to official colonization and in the next few years 6,032 additional ha were in private hands. A village, Saba'a Aioun,

---

[7] One of the landless Boukilis is Youssef. Youssef serves as a secretary to the elected sheikh of the Ait Harzallah and a general scribe for his own douar. In return for these services, the jma'a of the Harzallah allows him to cultivate two hectares (partially irrigated) on the plateau near his douar. An enterprising individual, Youssef bought an old sewing machine and taught himself to sew the traditional dresses of local women. He thus augments his income, especially during the winter months. In addition, Youssef's limited knowledge of reading and writing is put to lucrative use: he writes charms, concocts herbal medicines, and sells aphrodisiacs. Youssef became one of my informants; I joined his household for a period of three weeks to observe the role of women.

[8] I wish to thank M. A. Lahlimi for supplying me with maps and data on the Boubidman.

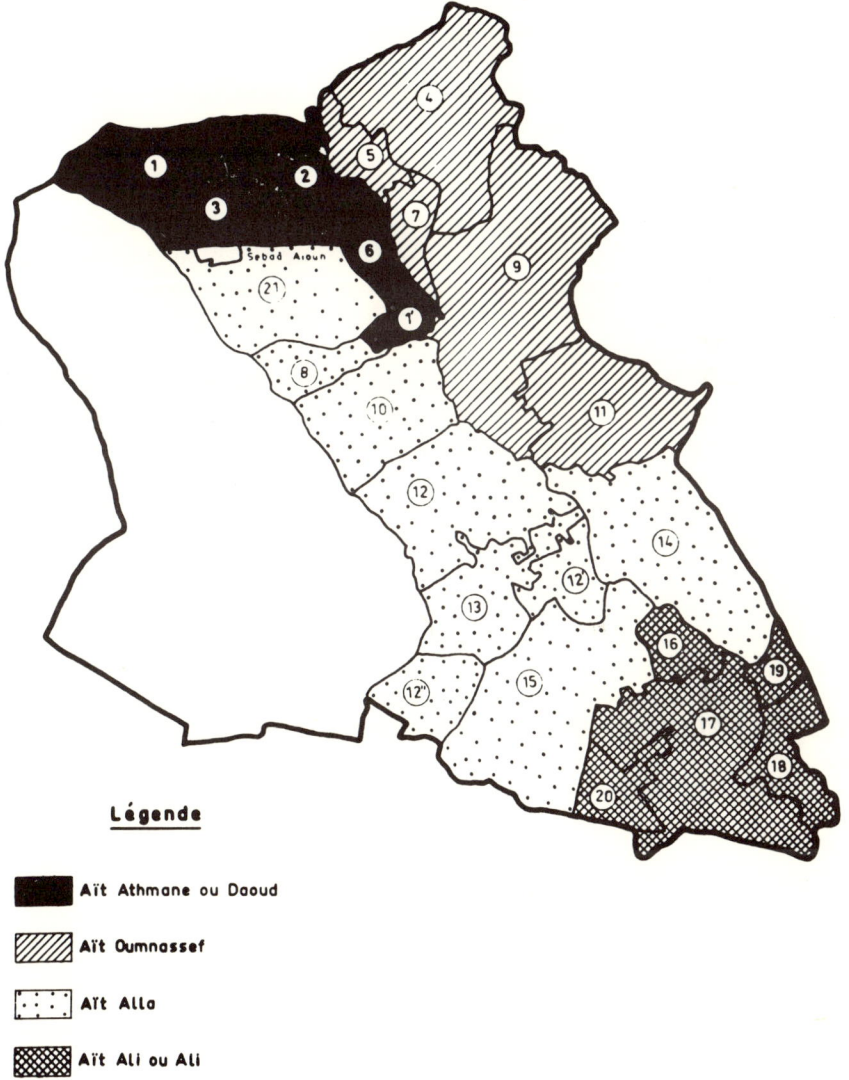

Fig. 10. Territorial division among the four factions, *ikhsan* of the Ait Boubidman prior to 1912.

was built by the French on the territory of the group to accommodate the laborers whom they imported from the Rif and Oujda. Many of these laborers ended up by buying land and settling among the Boubidman. An inquiry conducted by a Moroccan team in 1967 found that the Ait Boubidman totalled 12,146 people grouped into 1,938 households on an area that measured 13,400 ha. The density was 90.4 persons per square kilometer (as compared with 12 per sq. km in 1915). Of these 65 percent of the adult males were landless and of the remainder, 86 percent owned less than six ha of dry land.[9] Twenty percent of all the families derived all their income from salaried wage labor as farm hands on nearby estates.

The case of the Ait Boubidman highlights the major disjunctions present among the Ait Ndhir today. Concomitant with the amputation of their land there has occurred an increase in population. In 1950, the tribe numbered 70,000 (the census of 1960 lists a total of 82,000 Ait Ndhiri; the group had quadrupled in 50 years). Some of these were absorbed as wage laborers on the European farms. French patrons paid wages in cash every 15 days; however, the Moroccan government, which took over the official colon farms after independence, employs fewer workers. Individual Ndhiri seek work through patrons; of these the farm foreman, *cabran*, is very important in the countryside. However, even after work is found, the Ndhiri is not certain that he will get paid and some have waited as long as four months for their paychecks. The accounting in the provincial capital of Meknes, verification and cashing of checks, and the inefficient bureaucracy all delay payments. In March of 1967, unrest by unpaid farm workers in the region took the form of overt strikes. These however were quickly suppressed by the army.

UNANTICIPATED CONSEQUENCES: ARABIZATION AND RESIDUAL TRIBALISM

Whereas the Islamic invasion had succeeded in the moral conquest of Morocco, but fell short of total political control, the French accomplished a complete political takeover but failed in their efforts at a moral and cultural conquest of the peoples of Morocco. Religious and cultural differences were so great between the French and Moroccans that even the Berbers who were special targets of the "mission civilisatrice" failed to respond properly. Before examining the French cultural experiment with the Ait Ndhir, one must begin by restating and underlining the obvious: the single most potent agent for change was the establishment of a French administra-

---

[9]In this region, 12 ha are considered adequate for an average family of six people; two of these ha must be irrigated, *seguia*. A person who owns more than 50 ha is a large landowner; One with 30 ha is considered well-off, *sheb'an*. One third of the area must be irrigated.

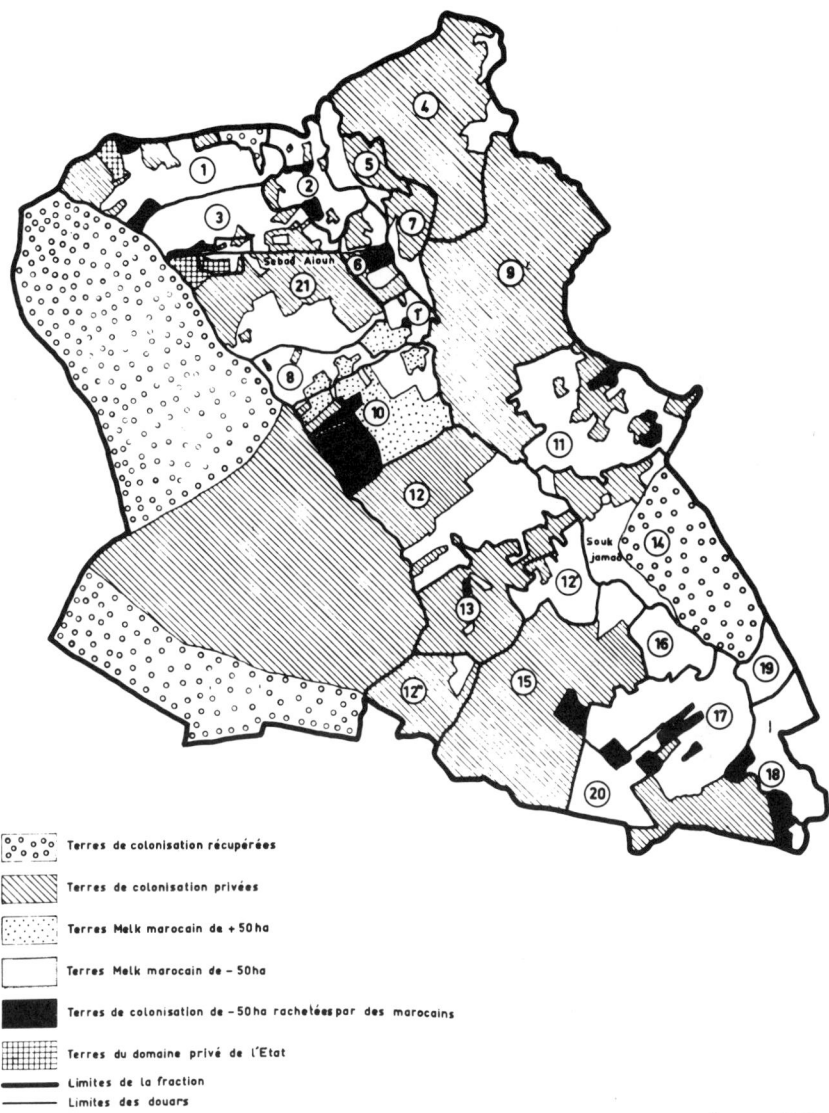

Fig. 11. Land ownership patterns in 1968 on territory of the Ait Boubidman.

tive system, backed by powerful coercive means, over all of Morocco. The Protectorate succeeded in altering the total political context of the country and thereby undermined the delicate balance between the makhzan and the tribes. The resulting detribalization process proceeded at different rates in the different areas;

among the Ait Ndhir, it occurred very early and unfolded with speed and brutality.[10]

In 1913, the Ait Ndhir tribe was divided into two administrative units, each comprised of six clans (the French added two tribal segments to the Ait Ndhir—Ait Ayash and Ait Lahsen ou Shaib): the Ait Ndhir of the North and the Ait Ndhir of the South. Qaids were appointed over each of the two divisions, the qaids having been chosen from among the leaders who had collaborated with the French during the war. The area of the tribe was declared a military region, circonscription, under the command of the political officers. The region was subject to French penal law and in civil affairs to the tribal customary law. A jma'a, whose members were coopted from the elected jma'as of the clans, served as a native court under the supervision of the controleur civil. The different customary laws, izref, of the clans were unified and written down in French in 1918.

Rather than substituting an expensive new administrative system, the French exploited the traditional political organization of the tribe and in doing so changed its character. The jma'a was limited by the French to the level of the clan, ighs; its duties were defined and the members were to be elected for a period of three years. This newly constituted oligarchic assembly came to serve as an intermediary body between the Protectorate and the tribe, an institution for the transmission of government directives rather than the original spontaneous defensive expression of the community. The new jma'a was placed in a bureaucratic structure; some of its traditional rights were confirmed while at the same time its freedom of action was restricted. The suppression of warfare and the takeover of the transhumance movements by the French officers undercut the original primary functions of the jma'as and rendered any supra-communal cooperation obsolete.

The authority of the administration over land titles became a powerful weapon for the punishment of those who were hostile to

---

[10]In addition to the amputation of tribal land by official and private appropriation, large areas on the plateau were delimited as forest preserves. By 1930, the officers in charge of the Ait Ndhir were seriously concerned over the massive migration to Meknes, growth of rural shanty-towns, as well as the general poverty and restlessness of the people. Quick palliatives were sought; one such scheme came to be known as "Bergeries Coopératives." The different clans of the Ait Ndhir were mobilized by the qaids and the officers to pool part of their livestock in newly-created cooperatives. These cooperatives were constructed and operated by obligatory corvée (the French prided themselves on having adapted two native institutions, collective ownership and the tiwizi, to new functions). Nevertheless, within two years the project had to be abandoned. Lack of financial support by the government and resistance of the tribesmen contributed to its failure. Part of the resistance was due to the fact that livestock was always considered individual property and Mtiris found it difficult to adjust to the idea of sharing their sheep and goats. For details on the "Bergeries Coopératives," see Boniface (1953:273-276), and Célérier (1936:209-237).

the regime and the reward of those who cooperated. Differential treatment of the jma'a members accelerated the socio-economic differentiations within the tribe and even within families. In time a petty class of notables emerged among the tribe.[11]

It was to this emerging class that the French directed their "politique berbère." In 1914, schools were founded near the military posts of El Hajeb, Ifran, and Agourai; officers took turns teaching French for a few hours each day. By 1923 l'École Franco-Berbère was established at El Hajeb and in 1926, a similar one was opened at Agourai. These schools were exclusively for Berbers and no Arabs were admitted. Their aim was to instruct the children of the local notables without detaching them from their rural milieu; all instruction was in French although a Latin alphabet was devised for writing Berber. The instructors hoped that the children would pass directly from Berber primitivism to French civilization without passing through the "intermediate" Arab stage.

The College d'Azrou was opened in 1927. Promising Berber students from all over Morocco were sent there and the outstanding graduates of the College entered the military school at Meknes. The colonizers prided themselves that in this way the independent warrior spirit of the Berber was being clothed in the best French cultural garb. These cadres were to go back to their tribes and disseminate French influence.

All these efforts notwithstanding, the Arab influence on the Ait Ndhir was steadily gaining ground. The security and roads established by the French, as well as the two new towns of Seba'a 'Aioun and Ain Taoujdat all served as the means for the encroachment of the Arab merchant, moneylender, and landlord on the Ait Ndhir territory. The newly sedentarized tribesman sold his wheat and vegetables to the Arab merchants, some of whom began to settle among the Berbers.

The upwardly mobile among the Ait Ndhir began to adopt the Arabic language and the urban customs, especially those of the inhabitants of Fez. The women, especially those in the towns, began to wear the veil and the *jellaba* (outer garment of dull color worn by urban Moroccan women) and learned to cook the cuisine of Fez. Bride price in cash, *sdaq*, began to be demanded and the financial arrangement in marriage imitated closely those of the Arabs in the

---

[11] This brief account of the Berber politics of the French in the region and its results is primarily based on Fuchs (1940), Thabault (1947), and Platon (1952).

Medina.[12] In short, those of the Ait Ndhir who could afford it, and many who could not, started to acquire the Arab urban life style. One wonders at the naivete of the French who expected the Berber to imitate the French style of life as represented by the rich patron and the political officer. Not only was it culturally alien, but it was economically prohibitive.

By failing to teach the Arabic language to the Berbers, the French prevented the majority from reading the Quran and helped to maintain the influence of the Arab shurfa. Actually despite the fact that the political roles of these shurfa, as mediators and arbitrators, was undermined by the Pax Gallica and the French officer, their socio-psychological functions, if anything, increased during the early years of the Protectorate. Intimidated by the French, confused by the new bureaucracy, and manipulated by the tribal leaders, the anxious and insecure Ndhiri turned to the shurfa and marabouts who served him as councillors, teachers, and physicians. By 1940, it became evident that the French had indirectly and unwittingly facilitated the gradual and pacific cultural conquest of the Ait Ndhir by the urban Arab.

Although the Ait Ndhir are almost completely detribalized today, some vestigial displays of an earlier life style remain. The tribal and clan names are used for identification and reference and the history of the tribe is recounted with pride and some nostalgia. The Ait Ndhir also participate in the obligatory ethnic displays put on by the government for the entertainment of kings and tourists. Those of the tribe who own fancy tents and horses are asked to demonstrate their allegiance to the king by parading in full ethnic regalia for two or three days a year. These artificial reunions of the tribes from all over the country serve to keep alive the tribal traditions in dance, song and dress. Old men gather together to reminisce and exchange stories; the young people challenge each other in song and dance. But to the majority these displays are merely a welcome diversion from their dull routine existence.

Another welcome diversion in which group solidarity may be displayed is the religious festival, *moussem*, which takes place at the local shrine. Collective pilgrimages to the shrine are arranged by the jma'as, money is collected and presented in the name of the clan, e.g., Ait Harzallah. The notables usually gather to offer a joint sacrifice which is followed by a ceremonial meal.

[12] In 1948, the jma'a of the Ait Ndhir decided to adopt the Moslem law, shari'a, in civil affairs; this allowed the women to inherit. Prior to 1948, the shari'a was voluntarily and selectively applied in the region which was considered a Berber area outside the jurisdiction of the Islamic legal codes.

Despite these few occasions where the Ait Ndhir manage to manifest some of their tribal heritage, today, in the midst of the most fertile area in Morocco, they exist as a dispossessed group of landless peasants and occasional wage laborers. Illiterate and insecure, the average Ndhiri leads a shiftless and haphazard existence, completely at the mercy of the local patrons, the notables of the region, and the representatives of the government. There is little planning ahead as daily life becomes a continuous improvisation. The present is not very attractive, the future not very promising. I found myself echoing the old men of the tribe who go around muttering *"Allah Yerham as-Siba"* ("Blessed were the old days").

VII

CONCLUSION

WITHIN the politically unstable and ecologically transitional area of the Meknes plateau during the period 1860-1912 there existed several rural groups that differed in their organizational response to the instability of the proximal central government, the makhzan. The rural groups comprised guish tribes, 'azibs, naiba, and independent tribes. This study focuses on the Ait Ndhir, one of the independent Berber tribes.

An examination of the history of the Ait Ndhir under the Alawi dynasty reveals the arbitrary and exploitative nature of the makhzan. The instability of the latter, coupled with its persistent and disruptive interference with the life of the tribe, led to the emergence of different adaptive mechanisms of socio-political organization. Foremost among these is nomadism, reflecting the need for mobility in the face of repeated military incursions by the makhzan and neighboring groups. Collective ownership of land served to preserve its integrity and provide the cohesiveness necessary to maintain the tribe as a politically viable, defensive entity. The lack of emphasis on agnatic affiliation and descent as the primary means for group recruitment and maintenance provided an additional flexibility in the response of the group to economic and political vicissitudes. The reconstruction of the sociopolitical organization of the Ait Ndhir prior to the Protectorate illustrates the workings of the foregoing mechanisms. The fragmentary information available for dir tribes (Ait Youssi, Seghrouchen, and Zayan) as well as other Middle Atlas tribes, suggests that the model generated for the Ait Ndhir may be of much wider application.

Although the Sais plain is fertile, the Ait Ndhir practiced limited agriculture in combination with transhumant nomadism. Their crops on the plain were vulnerable to attack by the makhzan; hence the high plateau served both as summer pasture and as a strategic retreat. Furthermore, the Ait Ndhir never developed permanent dwellings; they remained year round tent-dwellers. In contrast, the Ait Mguild, also transhumant, who were located to the south of the Ait Ndhir and thus farther away from the reach of the makhzan, inhabited stone dwellings during the winter months.

Tribal land was collectively owned, i.e. all adult resident males possessed equal rights to usufruct of the land which was never divided in mulk or sold. The only exception was the sale of small parcels by the tribal assembly to the shurfa, who played the important role of arbitrators of intratribal conflicts and mediators in intertribal confrontations. The agricultural part of the tribal land was divided among the camp units, tigemmis, the smallest subunit being the individual household. The pasture land was kept completely for communal usufruct. The seasonal transhumant migrations of the tigemmis required a substantial degree of coordination and cooperation among the leaders of the different primary segments of the tribe.

The organization and composition of the camp communities among the Ait Ndhir bear a striking resemblance to the corresponding levels of organization among the nomadic tribes of South Persia and West Pakistan, specifically the Basseri and Marri Baluch as analyzed by Fredrik Barth (1961) and Robert Pehrson (1966). This resemblance does not extend to the higher levels of political organization, namely, the tribe and its major sections. The groups of Southwest Asia possess centralized leadership, rigid political hierarchy and ranked lineages. Nobility among the Ait Ndhir was exclusive to the shurfa, leadership was situational and limited, and there was no ranking of the segments. Genealogies were not kept. These differences in social organization resulted from the different environments of the Middle Atlas Berbers and the multi-ethnic Southwest Asian populations. The consolidation of the power and wealth of the paramount leader of the Basseri is, largely, a result of his entrepreneurial and mediating role between the nomadic groups and the sedentary peasants whose villages and land are interspersed among the migratory routes of the pastoralists. The Ait Ndhir, in contrast, maintained no symbiotic relationship with any peasants, nor did their daily activities and nomadic migrations bring them into any sustained contact with different peoples.

Agnatic descent among the Ait Ndhir was only one variable in their social organization. Its primary function was to define the status and legitimacy of individuals and groups in terms of their access to resources. Group recruitment and maintenance was achieved by agnatic affiliation as well as through the institution of the sacrifice, tamghrost and the contractual institutions of the amḥars and amazẓal. Because of the abundance of land, the low tribal density, and continual defense needs, the Ait Ndhir displayed a relative lack of kin exclusiveness.

The advent of the French Protectorate altered completely the traditional sociopolitical makhzan-Ait Ndhir relationship. Massive acquisition of tribal land for agricultural colonization and the forced introduction of private property among the Ait Ndhir led to the breakdown of the tribal framework and resulted in the formation of a landless, anomic, rural proletariat.

APPENDIX I

The Ait Ndhir do not know how the expression "kaytir" became their name of Mtir or Ndhir; they simply say that it has to do with "us being fast like the bird who steals the grain and flies away." It is likely that the Arabic version of their name, Beni Mtir, was derived by prefixing the feminine particle of belonging, possession /m/, to the noun *tir* (bird). The feminine possessive in this case agrees in gender with the word *qabila*, or tribe; thus one gets *qabilat mtir*, or the tribe that is like the birds, or belongs to the birds.

APPENDIX II

Translation of a text in Berber gathered among the Ait Ndhir by Laoust (1939:265).

> When the people of the tribe all get together (*azdug* = reunion of all the camps of the tribe), the *amghar* tells them, "Beware, I do not want any fighting among you, no stealing and no hurting each other; you all have to obey and whoever fails to obey my commands will have to pay a fine (*izmam*) to the *jmaa* and his tent will be burned down." In other words, the people will go to his tent, they will kill his sheep, eat his food and then burn his tent down. If that person happens to be an *akhatar* (a notable, a respected man), he will quickly sacrifice a sheep to the *jmaa* and the people will go to the *amghar* and plead for him so that he will be spared.

APPENDIX III

The story of a famous tada between the clans of the Ait Iqeddaren and Ait Hammad as told by Hajj M. of Ait Iqeddaren in the summer of 1968 at El Hajeb:

> The *jmaa* of the *ikhsan* (clans) met in a large tent; they sacrificed sheep and ate a meal together. Then they called the *fqih* (religious teacher) and asked him to write down their *tada*. As soon as he finished writing,

the paper blew away into the sky. The old men present all stood up and said, 'God is great (Allah Akbar), this taḍa must be a blessed (mbarka) one for the angels took it.'" My informant then chuckled and added, "My father was present, and he knew that it was the wind that took the paper away and not the angels, but he did not want to say so and offend the religious old men of the tribe. And from that day on, this taḍa became known as the 'holy alliance,' eltada lmbarka.

APPENDIX IV

Translation of the text on taḍa (alliance) gathered among the Ait Ndhir and included in Laoust (1939):

> One day a *tigemmi* pulled up its tents and started to move to the summer pastures. As soon as they left, a man came from the direction of Fez. When he reached the area of decampment, he saw a chain lying on the ground, the kind that is used for horses and mules. He said to himself, "Here is a chain sent to me by God." But as soon as he bent to pick it up, it changed into a snake. He became frightened and ran back to his people and said, "Gather around me for I have something very strange to tell you: as I was walking on such and such a road, I found a chain, but as soon as I bent to pick it up, it changed into a snake." His people then told him, "That area (territory) belongs to Ait so and so who are our *ou taḍa*. Whoever among us trespasses on their boundaries or takes anything that belongs to them is punished by God. The snake was a warning to you."

APPENDIX V

The following is the text of the agreement between the representative of the French government and the jma'a of the Ait Ourtindi, a clan of the Ait Ndhir.

Acte de cession du Makhzen d'une portion du territoire des Ait Ourtindi (Beni Mtir).

La jmâa des Ait Ourtindi s'est réunie le 9 mars dans le bureau de renseignments de l'Annexe des Beni Mtir, à El Hajeb, en présence du caid Mohand ou Raho et du capitaine commandant l'Annexe.

Cette jmâa, composée de ... (suivent les noms des 17 membres), a écouté les propositions du glorieux gouvernement francais, transmises par le capitaine G., relatives à l'abandon au profit du Makhzen fortuné, Dieu augmente sa puissance, d'une partie du territoire de leur fraction.

Elle a pris acte de la promesse que cet abandon une fois consenti, les Ait Ourtindi recevraient, en toute propriété, à titre définitif et irrévocable, sous la garantie d'un dahir chérifien, le reste du territoire qu'ils ont recu de leurs ancêtres, qu'ils en pourraient opérer san délai le partage, afin que chacun recoive la part qui lui revient, fasse dresser pour cette part des actes lui en établissant la propriété individuelle et puisse disposer librement de ses biens, selon sa volonté et dans les délais et conditions fixés par le dahir sur la tutelle des collectivités.

Ils sollicitent instamment du glorieux Gouvernement français de prendre des mesures pour les mettre à l'abri des revendications ultérieures de tiers.

Les notables membres de la jmâa susmentionnés déclarent que, dans ces conditions, ils renoncent à tous leurs droits sur la portion du territoire de leur fraction désignée à la fin de l'acte et que cette cession est consentie sans paiement d'aucune indemnité, pour témoigner leur reconnaissance au glorieux Gouvernement français qui aurait pu leur prendre leurs terres au moment où ils ont fait leur soumission, ne leur a fait subir aucun préjudice dans leurs personnes et dans leurs biens et les a toujours traités avec bienveillance et bonté, comme un père traite ses enfants.

Ces déclarations ont été faites d'un commun accord par tous les membres de la jmâa susmentionnés et ont été revêtues de la signature du Caid Mohand ou Raho, Président de la jmâa de cette fraction.

The above statement was then followed by a detailed description of the land ceded by the group.

BIBLIOGRAPHY

Abes.
 1918 Les Aith Ndhir (publication du comité d'études berbères de Rabat). Editions Ernest Leroux. Paris.

Ader, Charles.
 1920 Le régime foncier marocain. Thèse pour le doctorat de sciences politiques. Toulouse.

Al-Hajji, Muhammad
 1964 Al-zawiya Al-dila'ya wadawruha Al-dini wal'ilmi walsiyasi. Rabat.

Al-Mawardi, Ali
 1960 Al-Ahkam Al-Suntaniya Walwilayat Al-Dinniyya. Egypt.

Al-Nasiri, Ahmad ibn Khaled
 1954- Al-istiqsa' li akhbar duwal al-maghrib al-aqsa, eds. Ja'far Al-Nasiri
 1959 and Muhammad Al-Nasiri. Casablanca.

Al-Zayyani, Abu al-Qasim
 1967 Al-Turjumanah al-Kubra, ed. Ahmad Fihali. Rabat.

Amar, E.
 1913 L'Organisation de la propriété foncière au Maroc: Etude théorique et practique. Paul Geuthner. Paris.

Arin, F.
 1914 "Essai sur les desmembrement de la propriété en droit musulman," Revue du monde musulman, vol. 26:277-317.

Arnaud, Commt. Ed.
 1916 "La région de Meknès," Bull. de la société de géographie du Maroc, no. 2:47-105.

Arnaud, Louis
 1952 Au temps des "méhallas" ou le Maroc de 1860 à 1912. Editions Atlantides. Casablanca.

Aubin, Eugéne
 1904 Le Maroc d'aujourd'hui. Librairie Armand Colin. Paris.

Ayache, A.
 1956 Le Maroc: bilan d'une colonisation. Paris.

Barth, Fredrik.
 1961 Nomads of South Persia; The Basseri Tribe of the Khamseh Confederacy. Humanities Press. New York.

Bernard, Augustin
 1909 "La propriété immobilière au Maroc," Congrès de l'Afrique du Nord, vol. 2:740-750.

Berque, Jacques
   1937 "Sur un coin de terre marocaine: seigneurs terriens et paysans," Ann. d'Hist. Econ. et Soc., no. 45:227-235.
   1950 "Petits documents d'histoire sociale marocaine: les archives d'un cadi rural," Revue Africaine, 94, pp. 113-124.
   1953 "Qu'est-ce qu'une "tribu" nord-africaine?" Eventail de l'histoire vivante—Hommage à Lucien Febvre, vol. 1:260-271.
   1955 Structures sociales du Haut Atlas. Paris.
   1957 "Quelques problèmes de l'islam Maghrébin," Archives de sociologie des religions, 2nd year, pp. 3-20.
   1958 "Droit des terres et integration sociale au Maghreb," Cahiers internationaux de sociologie, 25, pp. 38-74.
   1962 "Sciences sociales et décolonisation," Tiers-Monde, vol. 3, no. 9-10, pp. 1-15.

Brignon, J., et. al.
   1967 Histoire du Maroc. Casablanca.

Brisset, Pierre
   N.D. Rites agraires et moussems dans les Beni Mtir. Rabat, 64 p. dactylo.

Brunot, Emile
   1953 L'exercise de la Chefâa et la préemption devant jurisdictions françaises du Maroc. Thèse. Bordeaux: (dactylo).

Bruno, Henri
   1918 "Introduction à l'étude du droit coutumier des berberes du Maroc Central," Archives Berbères, vol. 3, fasc. 4, pp. 297-309.

Bruno, H. et G. H. Bousquet
   1946 "Contributions à l'étude des pactes de protection et d'alliance chez les berbères au Maroc Central," Hespéris, vol. 33:353-357.

Burke, Edmund
   1968 "The Tribal Factor in North African History: The Ait Ndir and Morocco, 1900-1914." Unpublished paper delivered at the Middle East Studies Association Conference, Austin, Texas.

Célérier, J.
   1927 "La transhumance dans le Moyen-Atlas," Hespéris, vol. 7: 00-00.
   1936 "Chez les berbères du Maroc: de la collectivité patriarcale à la coopérative," Annales d'histoire économique et sociale, no. 39:210-237.
   1938 "L'évolution de la propriété foncière dans une tribu marocaine: du régime collectif à l'individualisation," Revue Africaine, no. 81:247-283.
   1938 "La montagne au Maroc (Essai de définition et de classification)," Hespéris, vol. 25:109-180.
   1939 "Histoire rurale et colonisation indigène au Maroc," Communication faite au 5me Congrès de la Fédération des Soc. Savantes de l'Afrique du Nord. Tunis.

Colin, G. S.
   1938 "Origine arabe des grands mouvements des populations berbères dans le Moyen Atlas," Hespéris, vol. 38:265-268.

Courageot, Pierre
   1934 Les communautés agraires du Maroc et le Protectorat français. Thèse. Toulouse.

Dermenghen, Emile
   1954 Le culte des saints dans l'Islam Maghrébin. Paris.

Desme de Cyavigny
    1911   La terre collective de tribu en Algérie et en Tunisie. Tunis.

Despois, Jean
    1954   L'Afrique du Nord, 3rd ed. Paris.

Doutté, Edmond
    1905   "L'organisation domestique et sociale chez les H'ah'a," Rens. Col. pp. 1-16.
    1914   En tribu. Paris.

Drague, Georges
    1951   Esquisse d'histoire religieuse du Maroc. Paris.

Favret, Jeanne
    1968   "La segmentarité au Maghreb," L'Homme, vol. 6, no. 2, pp. 105-111.

Foucauld, Charles de
    1939   Reconnaissance au Maroc en 1883-1884. Conforme à l'édition de 1888 et augmenté de fragments inédits rédigés par l'auteur pour son cousin Français de Bondy. Paris.

Gadille, J.
    1955   "La colonisation officielle au Maroc," Cah. d'Outre-Mer, no. 32, pp. 305-322.

Gaillard, Henri
    1909   "L'administration au Maroc: le Makhzen, étendue et limites de son pouvoir," Bulletin de la Société de Géographie d'Alger, 14, pp. 438-470.
    1919   "L'état Marocain," in Villes et tribus du Maroc, vol. IV, part II. Paris.

Gand, Jean
    1942   "Quelques données démographiques sur trois fractions de la tribu Beni Mtir," Bulletin de l'institut d'hygiène du Maroc, vol. 2:79-91.

Gay, F.
    1929   "Csutumes berbères et droit musulman comparés. Essai sur la priété familiale en pays de coutumes berbères et en pays de Chra," Revue alg. tun. et mar. de légis. et de juris. pp. 187-195.

Gellner, Ernest
    1969   Saints of the Atlas. Weidenfeld and Nicolson. London.

────── and Charles Micaud, eds.
    1973   Arabs and Berbers. London

Guillaume, Albert
    1960   La propriété collective au Maroc. (Coll. etudes jurid. pol. et économique de l'Université du Maroc, no. 8) Rabat.

Guillaume, Augustin
    1946   Les berbères marocaines et la pacification de l'Atlas Central (1912-1933). Paris.

Harris, Walter B.
    1895   The Narrative of a Journey of Information in the Atlas Mountains and the Oasis of the North West Sahara. London.
    1897   "The Nomadic Berbers of Central Morocco," Geographical Journal, vol. 9:638-645.

Hart, D. M.
   1973   The Tribe in Modern Morocco: Two Case Studies, *In*: Arabs and Berbers, E. Gellner and C. Micaud, eds. London.

Huot, (Col.)
   1928   "Les terres collectives et la colonisation Européenne au Maroc," Afrique Française, Rens. Col. pp. 277-292.

Ibn-Khaldun, Abdel-Rahman
   1956-   Kitab Al-'ibar. 7 vols. Beirut.
   1960

Irons, William George
   1969   The Yomut Turkomen: A Study of Kinship in a Pastoral Society. Ph.D. dissertation, Department of Anthropology, University of Michigan.

Jacquet et Franqueira
   1934   "La révision des biens Guich et des terres collectives," Gazette des tribunaux du Maroc, 24 fev., pp. 57-88.

Khalil Ibn Ishaq, Al Jundi
   1973   Maliki Law; being a summary from the French translation of the Mukhtasar with notes and bibilography by F. H. Ruxton. London.

Khatibi, Abdelkabir
   1969   Bilan de la sociologie au Maroc. Publications de l'Association pour la Recherche des Sciences Humaines. Rabat.

Lahlimi, Ahmad
   1967   "Quelques réflexions sur les collectivités rurales traditionelles et leur évolution," Bulletin économique et social du Maroc, vol. 26: 59-83.

Lapanne-Joinville, J.
   1959   Note sur le régime foncier musulman (rite malkite). Dactylo. Rabat.

Latron, A.
   1938   "Problème foncier et bled marocain: évolution d'un groupement rural dans une tribu berbère, les Beni Mtir," L'Afrique Française, mars, pp. 124-128 et avril, pp. 176-180.

Lazarev, Grigori
   1968   "Les concessions foncières au Maroc. Contribution à l'étude de la formation des domaines personnels dans les campagnes marocaines," Annal's marocain's de sociologie, vol. 1:99-135.

Lazarev, G. et P. Pascon
   1962   "Les caractéristiques des exploitations agricoles," Hommes, Terre et Eau, no. 2:53-87.

Leclère (chef de batallion)
   1922   Terres collectives de tribu. Direction des affaires indigènes et du service des renseignements.

Le Coz, Jean
   1964   Le Rharb; fellahs et colons, tomes I et II. Rabat.

Lesne, M.
   1959   Histoire d'un groupement berbère, les Zemmour. Rabat.

Lewis, William H.
   1961   "Feuding and Social Change in Morocco," Journal of Conflict Resolution, vol. 5:43-54.

Magnin, Jean
    1952 "Note sur les alliances traditionelles dans le Moyen-Atlas septentrional," Anthropos, 47, pp. 784-794.

Mansour, Abdel Wahab ben
    1968 Qaba'il al-Maghrib, vol. I. Royal Press. Rabat.

Marcais, Georges
    1946 La Berbérie musulmane et l'orient au moyen age. Paris.

Marcy, G.
    1929 "Une tribu berbère de la confédération Ait Warain: les Ait Jellidasen," Hespéris, vol. 9:79-142.
    1936 "L'alliance par collactation (tada) chez les berbères du Maroc Central," Revue Africaine, vol. 2:957-973.
    1949 Le droit coutumier Zemmour. Paris.

Marty, Paul
    1928 "Droit coutumier berbère: L'orf des Beni Mtir (orf unifie dans une assemblée générale des djemmaas en avril 1918)," Revue des Etudes Islamiques, vol. 4:485-511.

Mauduit, R.
    1903 "Le Makhzen Marocain," Afrique Française, Rens. Col., 12, pp. 293-304.

Mesurer, A.
    1921 La propriété foncière du Maroc. Paris.

Michaux-Bellaire, E.
    1908 "La maison d'Ouazzan," Revue de Monde Musulman, vol. 5, no. 5, pp. 22-89.
    1908 "Les biens habous et les biens makhzen, à point de vue de leur alienation," Revue de Monde Musulman, vol. 5:436-457.
    1909 "Les coutumes berbères dans les tribus arabes," Revue du Monde Musulman, vol. 9:224-234.
    1911 "Le territoire makhzen et le territoire guich, Revue du Monde Musulman, vol. 15:74-89.
    1914 "Une tentative de restauration idrisite à fes," Revue du Monde Musulman, vol. 5:393-395.

Michaux-Bellaire, E. et G. Salmon
    1905 "Les tribus arabes de la vallee du Lekkous," Archives marocaines, vol. 4:1-151.

Miège, J. L.
    1961- Le Maroc et l'Europe (1830-1894). Vol. 1: Sources, bibliographie;
    1962 vol. 2: L'ouverture; vol. 3: Les difficultés. Paris.

Milliot, Louis
    1922 Les terres collectives, étude de législation marocaine. Paris.

Ministère des Finances, Rabat.
    1956 Nomenclature des tribus et fractions des tribus.

Montagne, Robert
    1924 "Une tribu berbère du sud marocain: Massat," Hespéris, vol. 4:357-403.
    1927 "Organisation sociale et politique des tribus berbères indépendentes," Revue des Etudes Islamiques, vol. 2:223-247.
    1930 Les berbères et le makhzen dans le sud de Maroc. Paris.

Nicolas, Georges
    1961   "La sociologie rurale au Maroc," Tiers-Monde, vol. 2, no. 8 pp. 527-543.

Pehrson, Robert N.
    1966   The Social Organization of the Marri Baluch, compiled and analyzed from Pehrson's notes by Fredrik Barth. "Viking Fund Publications in Anthropology," no. 43. New York: Wenner-Gren Foundation for Anthropological Research.

Piersuis.
    1941   Etude sur les communautés rurales des Beni Ansen. Moncho. Rabat.

Platon, Paul
    1950   "Le mouton chez les berbères Beni Mtir de la région d'El Hadjeb," 33 pages (dactylo). El-Hadjeb.
    1947   "La culture du mais chez les Beni Mtir," Bulletin de l'enseignement public du Maroc, pp. 100-123.
    1952   "Le jardinier ou 'rebaa' chez les Beni Mtir de la région d'El Hadjeb," Bulletin de l'enseignment public du Maroc, 2 trim. pp. 107-110.

Protectorat de la Republique Francaise au Maroc—Gouvernement chérifien. Direction Generale de l'agriculture, du commerce, et de la colonisation. Le dévelopment du régime foncier au Maroc.

Quendenfeldt, M.
    1902   "Division et répartition de la population berbère au Maroc," Revue
    1903   Africaine, vol. 46:263-301; vol. 47:134-170, 264-303, and 372-382;
    1904   vol. 48:134-170.

Recoules, Jean
    1960   "'Siba' au Maroc," L'Afrique et l'Asie, vol. 51:13-19.

Salmon, G.
    1904   "Les institutions berbères au Maroc," Archives Marocaines, vol. 1: 127-148.
    1904   "Quelques particularités de la propriété foncière dans le R'arb," Archives Marocaines, vol. 2:144-149.
    1905   "Essai sur l'histoire politique du Nord Marocain," Archives Marocaines, vol. 2:1-99.
    1905   "Le Tertib," *Archives Marocaines*, vol. 2, pp. 154-158.

Segonzac, Marquis de
    1903   Voyages au Maroc (1888-1901). Paris.

Surdon, Georges
    1926   "Les terres collectives," Gazette des Tribunaux du Maroc, no. 4 fev., 1 et 15 avril, 6 et 20 mai.
    1928   Esquisses de droit coutumier berbère marocain. Rabat.
    1931   La justice civile indigène et le régime de la propriete immobilière au Maroc. Moncho. Rabat.

Szymanski, ed.
    1970   "Les tribus de 'guich' et le makhzen," Revue de l'Occident Musulman et de la Medit. numéro special, pp. 195-202.

Tassoni, (Lt.)
    1928   "Contributions à l'étude du régime coutumier des terres collectives. Les terres de djemaa au Maroc," Revue alger., tunis., et maroc. de législation et de juris. pp. 100-124 et pp. 133-157.

Terrasse, Henri
    1950   Histoire du Maroc des origines à l'établissement du protectorat fançais. 2 vols. Casablanca.

Thaubault, Albert
    1947 L'influence fançaise sur l'évolution sociale des Guerouanes du sud et des Beni Mtir. (circons. de controle civile d'El Hadjeb), mem. de stage, 1947 (dactylo) 64 pp.
Vermeil
    1928 La situation juridique de terres en pays Beni Mtir. (mem. de fin de stage des contrôles civiles), promotion de 1928. El Hadjeb.
Waterbury, John
    1970 The Commander of the Faithful, the Moroccan Elite: A Study in Segmented Politics. Weiddenfeld and Nicolson. London.
Zaydan, ben Abderahman
    1961 Al'zz wal Sawla fi Ma'alim nuḍum al Dawla, vol. I and II. Rabat.

PLATE 1. A douar.

PLATE 2. An isolated household.

PLATE 3. A summer camp of the Ait Ndhir.

PLATE 4. Ait Ndhir tribesmen participating in a Fantasia.

PLATE 5. A ceremonial tent in the Middle Atlas Mountains.

PLATE 6. Holiday costume of an Ndhiri girl.

PLATE 7. The fqih and his family. Ait Harzallah.

PLATE 8. The former qaid of the Ait Ndhir and his wife in ceremonial dress.

PLATE 9. The Monday market near El-Hajeb.

PLATE 10. Market scene.

PLATE 11. The market near El-Hajeb.

PLATE 12. Going home from the market.